The Celebrity Cook Book

© The Leukaemia and Cancer Children's Fund

in association with

CALEDONIAN PUBLISHING LTD

"ENJOY OUR CELEBRITY COOK BOOK"

A Book with a difference – Over the past two years, we at the Fund office in Edinburgh have been beavering away collecting recipes from all corners of the world. Stars from Stage, Screen, Television, Sport and Politics have helped to make this a most enterprising challenge to one and all. The funds raised from the sale of the book will considerably enhance the wellbeing of the children. They will go to equip Buchanan House of Recovery Holiday/Caring Centre. We are delighted that as the house is in Blairgowrie it will allow the children great freedom, fresh air, fishing, berry picking and family walks, no family is turned away. Children from Scotland, England, Wales and Ireland will benefit. "You" by purchasing this Cook Book will be helping those who cannot help themselves (If I can help somebody along the way my living has not been in vain).

Aye in faith.

Dame Denise Brett MBE. DLJ.
Director Leukaemia and Cancer Children's Fund.

First published in 1988 by Caledonian Publishing Limited,
John Cotton Building, Edinbugh,
on behalf of the Leukaemia & Children's Fund.

ISBN 0/951 3926/03
Designed by Alan White Associates
typeset by ex-height
Printed and bound in Scotland by Holmes MacDougall.

Contents

Conversion Tables

More than 130 celebrities from around the world have contributed to this book. Time and the great British postal strike of 1988 have prevented us from standardising units of measurement throughout the text. We hope that when you use the book this will not detract from your enjoyment of the many recipes.

The following are approximate conversions, which have been either rounded up or down. We may have mixed metric and imperial throughout the book, but we'd advise you never to mix the two in one recipe; stick to one system or the other.

WEIGHTS		VOLUME		MEASUREMENTS	
½ oz	10 g	1 fl oz	25 ml	¼ inch	0.5 cm
1	25	2	50	½	1
1½	40	3	75	1	2.5
2	50	5(¼ pint)	150	2	5
3	75	10(½)	275	3	7.5
4	110	15(¾)	400	4	10
5	150	1 pint	570	6	15
6	175	1¼	700	7	18
7	200	1½	900	8	20.5
8	225	1¾	1 litre	9	23
9	250	2	1.1	11	28
10	275	2¼	1.3	12	30.5
12	350	2½	1.4		
13	375	2¾	1.6	OVEN TEMPERATURES	
14	400	3	1.75	Mark 1 275°F	140°C
15	425	3¼	1.8	Mark 2 300	150
1 lb	450	3½	2	Mark 3 325	170
1¼	550	3¾	2.1	Mark 4 350	180
1½	700	4	2.3	Mark 5 375	190
2	900	5	2.8	Mark 6 400	200
3	1.4 kg	6	3.4	Mark 7 425	220
4	1.8	7	4.0	Mark 8 450	230
5	2.3	8(1 gal)	4.5	Mark 9 475	240

Thanks.

Many people have given freely of their time or donated services far in excess of their usual fees in order that this book might be produced. The Leukaemia and Cancer Children's Fund would like to express its very special thanks to TV am and Anne Diamond, Russell Grant, Gordon Honeycombe and Jane Irving, Bete Gibson and Nessie Bryant (volunteer workers at the Fund's Edinburgh headquarters), Arthur Reid (for interupting his schedule for Punch magazine to ensure that the illustrations were completed on time), Maria Whittaker for giving so freely of her time and energy, and to Photo Express.

WHEN IT COMES TO CHOOSING THE RIGHT BANK MAKE SURE YOU'RE LOOKING IN THE RIGHT DIRECTION.

Banking Services

Does your bank respond to your needs as quickly as it might? Or is it taking too long to make vital decisions?

If so, it could be time you started looking around for a better service.

Look no further.

At The Royal Bank of Scotland we believe we can offer you that better service, because we're prepared to go out of our way to help you in any way we can.

So why not come in and see us?

We don't regard ourselves as just another bank. That's why we won't regard you as just another customer.

IT ALL POINTS TO THE ROYAL BANK OF SCOTLAND

The Royal Bank of Scotland

Registered office: 36 St Andrew Square, Edinburgh EH2 2YB. Registered in Scotland No. 90312.

A Member of IMRO and of AFBD

JUNE'S JUICE

June Whitfield

INGREDIENTS

1 litre tomato juice.
juice of 2 oranges.
juice of 1 lemon.
grated skin of 1 orange.

Boil ingredients together for 5 minutes. Strain and add 1 dessertspoon Worcester sauce.

"I was serving kebabs to my guests and easing the meat and vegetables off the first skewer onto a plate. I sadly missed and the whole lot went on the floor. Quite a moment to remember."

KIPPER PATE

—— Serves 6 ——

INGREDIENTS

6 oz kipper fillets.
4 oz cottage cheese.
2 oz melted butter.
1 tablespoon lemon juice.
1 tablespoon Worcester sauce.
3 tablespoons melted butter (for finish).

Remove skin and any large bones from kippers. Place kippers, cottage cheese, melted butter and lemon juice into blender, liquidise. Spoon into small dishes, seal with melted butter, chill and serve.

Will freeze well.

POTTED HOUGH WITH BABY BEETROOT SAUCE

INGREDIENTS

1 lb of hough.
1 nap bone.
2 oz butter.
chopped parsley.
2 – 3 baby beetroots.
black pepper.

Boil the hough and the nap bone together for 2 – 3 hours until meat is tender. Remove from the stock, mince the mutton, remove the marrow from the nap bone. Place the mutton and marrow back in the stock and reboil. Pour into required dishes and seal with the melted butter, place in fridge and allow to set. Serve the potted hough with the baby beetroot and garnish with chopped parsley and plenty black pepper.

HRH *Princess Alexandra*

Capital Hotel, Edinburgh

Head Chef – DOUGLAS MACDONALD
Senior Sous Chef – BREMNER MACDONALD

MACKEREL MOUSSE

INGREDIENTS

1 lb (450 g) tin mackerel (for a more splendid occasion use a tin of salmon).
2 sticks of celery (finely chopped).
1 tablespoon capers.
¼ pint (150 ml) double cream (whipped).
pepper and salt to taste.
1 teaspoon dry mustard.
1 teaspoon powdered gelatine.
1 tablespoon wine vinegar.
3 tablespoons water.
1 tablespoon sugar.
a fish or ring mould.

Mix together the first five ingredients in a bowl.

Either put remainder in a non-stick saucepan and gently heat until gelatine has dissolved – or put ingredients in small heatproof bowl, place in boiling water – lower the heat and simmer until gelatine dissolves. Pour liquid into bowl with other ingredients and mix well. Wet mould under cold water. Spoon ingredients in and place in fridge to set.

Can be decorated by putting a layer of tomato or cucumber on bottom of mould.

This is an ideal dish to freeze.

SALMON MOUSSE

— Serves 4 —

INGREDIENTS

2   7½ oz tins salmon.
1 pint double cream.
½ oz gelatine.
1 lemon.
¼ pint water.

Take blackskins off the salmon and any black bits and loosen it up. Add grated lemon peel, lemon juice, salt and black pepper. Beat cream till stiff. Fold in salmon and gelatine (melted).

Set in fish dish.

Jan Leeming

Roy Kinnear

IBM in Scotland-more than three decades of growth.

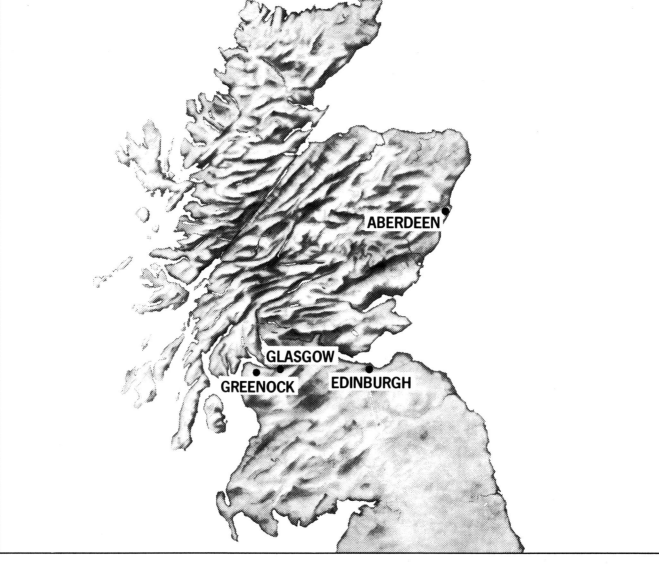

IBM has been an integral part of the Scottish economy since 1951–the year IBM United Kingdom was formed. That year, IBM UK established its first manufacturing plant at Greenock on the banks of the Clyde, where 100 people built typewriters and accounting machines.

Today, 2,700 people work there producing advanced information technology products including Display Systems and the IBM Personal Computer. Over 85 per cent of IBM Greenock's production is exported to countries in Europe, the Middle East and Africa.

Through branch offices in Edinburgh, Glasgow and Aberdeen, IBM UK serves more than 4,000 Scottish customers; from banking and insurance to North Sea oil and gas; from manufacturing to retailing and distribution; from education to local and central government administration.

IBM's operations in Scotland, those of our customers and of the 2,000 British suppliers to the Greenock plant, contribute significantly to the prosperity and welfare of Scotland and to the economy as a whole.

IBM UNITED KINGDOM LIMITED, BUCHAN HOUSE, 21 ST. ANDREW SQUARE, EDINBURGH EH2 1AY.

Soup

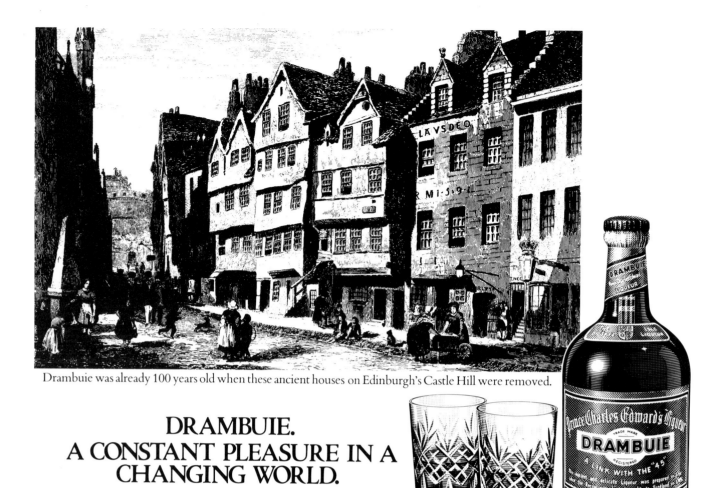
A RECIPE FROM THE ROXBURGHE

We are happy to donate to this very special book the recipe for a rich and rewarding crepe inspired by a Bonnie Prince.

This is one of our chef's favourite dishes which he delights in creating for discerning diners at our elegant hotel in the heart of Edinburgh.

BON APPETIT!

PRINCE CHARLES EDWARD CREPE

INGREDIENTS
4 Large crepes of a basic recipe
1 Large chopped onion
1 Medium cooked and diced veal sweetbread
10oz of diced raw breast of chicken
1 x 5oz goblet of Drambuie
1 x 5oz goblet of double cream
10oz of Bechamel or white sauce
2oz branch parsley
Juice of 2 limes
3oz softened butter

METHOD
Melt one ounce of the butter and saute the onions gently until transparent. Add the diced chicken and cook for 4 minutes then add the sweetbread and cook for a further minute. Pour in the Drambuie, bring to the boil and continue boiling until the liquid is reduced. Stir in half the cream and half of the Bechamel or white sauce and boil for 2–3 minutes. Add the lime juice and allow the mixture to cool slightly.
Divide the filling evenly between the crepes, roll up and place in a warm serving dish. Bring the remaining cream and Bechamel sauce to the boil, then remove from the heat and stir in the remaining butter. Pour the sauce over the crepes and garnish with pastry.

The Roxburghe Hotel

Charlotte Square, Edinburgh EH2 4HG Telephone: 031-225 3921

BASIL SOUP

——————— Serves 8 ———————

Put 2 litres of water in a saucepan and the following chopped vegetables.

1 lb string beans and white beans.
3 or 4 potatoes and carrots.
2 peeled zucchini.

Season with salt and pepper and simmer. Fifteen minutes before all the vegetables are cooked, add 3-4 tablespoons of noodles.

In a separate bowl, crush 2-3 garlic cloves, to which you add chopped basil. Add half a glass of olive oil, mix thoroughly and sprinkle with grated cheese. Mix soup with this preparation and serve.

CARROT SOUP

INGREDIENTS

3 large carrots, peeled and sliced.
1 oz butter or margarine.
2 oz flour.
$1/2$-$3/4$ pint boiling water.
milk if necessary.

Cook the carrots in the butter or margarine for about 5 minutes. Add the flour and stir for 2 minutes to make a roux. Mix in the boiling water. Leave to simmer for 25-30 minutes or until the carrots are soft.

Remove from heat and liquidise. If the mixture is too thick add milk.

Season to taste, heat and serve.

The Royal Family of Monaco

Ian Paisley MP

CARROT AND ORANGE SOUP

INGREDIENTS

12 oz carrots.
2 large oranges.
1½ oz butter.
2 medium onions.
1 bayleaf.

Sweat carrots and onions. Add 1½ pints good stock. Add zest of 1 orange. Simmer until soft. Liquidise or put through sieve. Pour in orange juice and reheat.

This soup is also delicious cold (for the Summer).

CHILLED TOMATO SOUP

This reflects my vegetarian tastes. I haven't eaten meat for over 10 years and the recipe below is delicious and totally acceptable to all eaters with the exception of those who don't eat tomatoes.

INGREDIENTS

2 14 oz cans of tomatoes.
1 garlic clove.
a few fresh basil leaves (or a little dried).
2 teaspoons lemon juice.
1 teaspoon sugar.
salt and pepper.
2 cartons soured cream.

Put into blender ½ can of tomatoes, together with lemon juice, sugar, basil, salt and pepper and the garlic, crushed into a little salt. Blend until quite smooth. Then add the rest of the tomatoes with their juices and blend again.

Denis Healey

Nigel Hawthorne

Next blend in the cartons of soured cream. When it is smooth and creamy, check it for seasoning. Adjust to taste if needed. Pour into a bowl or separate bowls and refrigerate until very cold. Cover the bowl.

As you can see, if you want to make half the quantity it is an easy recipe to split down the middle.

GREEN PEA SOUP

David Jacobs

—————— Serves 4 ——————

INGREDIENTS

1 lb packet frozen peas.
1 lettuce heart sliced.
bunch spring onions chopped.
2 slices ham diced.
2 pints stock (made with stock cube).
handful of fresh mint.
butter.
2 tablespoons sugar.

Soften the onions in the butter, add peas, lettuce, ham and sugar. Simmer for 10 minutes. Stir to avoid burning. Add the stock and the mint. Simmer for another 10 minutes. Season and mix in blender, to required thickness.

If a thinner soup is preferred add a little more stock.

This soup freezes well and is good hot or cold. Serve with a little cream on top, chopped mint and fried croutons.

ICED CURRY CREAM SOUP (CRÈME CONSTANCE)

INGREDIENTS

4 oz finely chopped shallots.
1 oz butter.
1 level tablespoon curry paste.
1 oz flour.
1³/₄-2 pints vegetable or chicken stock.
1 strip of lemon rind.
1 small bay leaf.
1 small dessert spoon arrowroot.
cream (see below).

Soften shallots in ³/₄ oz of butter, then add curry paste. Cook for 4-5 minutes. Add the rest of the butter, then the flour and pour on the stock. Bring to the boil, add lemon rind and bayleaf, simmer for 20 minutes, strain and return to the rinsed pan to reduce if necessary. Then add the arrowroot slaked with a tablespoon of cold water and reboil. Strain again, cool, then chill. Serve with a spoonful of the following cream in each cup.

CREAM
1 wineglass port.
1 teaspoon curry paste or powder.
1 good dessert spoon apricot jam or puree from dried apricots.
2 tablespoons whipped cream or evaporated milk.

Mix the port and curry paste or powder together and simmer until reduced to half quantity. Leave till cold. Mix with the puree or jam. strain, then beat into the cream

Derek Nimmo

"Food, I think, is very important for the success of a happy marriage. I myself have been married for 33 years. We got engaged 34 years ago in a little restaurant in Soho. After all these years, we still return there once a month. My wife goes on Mondays and I go on Fridays."

PARSNIP SOUP

Rt Hon Nigel Lawson MP

This soup has become a firm favourite of ours – and I find it useful when entertaining, as it has never gone wrong. It can also be quite a conversation piece since hardly anybody has ever managed to identify the main ingredient.

INGREDIENTS

3 oz butter.
a very large parsnip.
4 oz finely chopped onion.
clove garlic (crushed or finely chopped).
1 tablespoon flour.
1 teaspoon good quality curry powder.
2 pints hot beef stock.
¼ pint cream.
chives to garnish if available.

Peel and slice parsnip and cook it very gently in a heavy saucepan with the butter, onion and garlic keeping the lid on. The vegetables shouldn't brown, just soften. Add the flour and curry powder to take up the fat, stirring with a wooden spoon, and gradually incorporate the hot stock. Simmer until the parsnip is cooked. Allow to cool slightly then blend until smooth. Return to saucepan, correct seasoning (add salt, pepper and a bit more curry powder if required), and then stir in the cream, decant the soup and sprinkle the chives (if available) over the top.

Serve with croutons.

LEEK AND POTATO SOUP

Cliff Richard

——— Serves 6 ———

INGREDIENTS

2 pints chicken stock.
2 onions.
1 lb potatoes.
1/2 lb leeks.
mixed herbs.
2 oz butter.
1/4 pint natural yogurt.

Peel potatoes and cut into small chunks. Chop onions roughly. Cut leeks into segments.

Melt the butter in a large pan and saute the potatoes and onions for a few minutes. Add the stock, herbs and leeks. Simmer until potatoes are cooked. Allow to cool for ten minutes.

Mix in the yogurt, then put the soup through a blender at maximum speed.

Serve hot/cold

From the horse's mouth

A COMPLETELY UNSOLICITED testimonial appeared recently in A La Carte, the definitive mouthpiece of food and wine.

It was penned by Raymond Gardner and it concerned *"...the superbly mellow Macallan from Craigellachie in Banffshire, aged in sherry casks, a mellow miracle and to my mind the most sophisticated of the commonly-available Highland malts..."*

If that is what the pundits think, perhaps it is time to let your own mouthpiece pronounce on the subject.

THE MACALLAN. THE MALT.

ASSIETTE DE FRUITS DE MER MOSCOVITE

—————— Serves 4 ——————

INGREDIENTS

8 French langoustine.
1 fresh trout.
4 oz fresh salmon.
8 mussels.
8 queen scollops.
4 squid (small).
1 teaspoon Beluga caviar.
1 teaspoon Keta caviar.
1 pinch saffron stamen.
4 dl double cream.
1 dl white wine.
1 dl fish stock.
1 oz shallots (chopped).
4 oz seaweed.
2 oz butter.

Cut salmon and trout into diamonds, season all fish and mark with a skewer.

Heat 1 oz butter in a pan and sweat shallots; add ½ dl fish stock and cook washed mussels and scollops until the shells open. Take out mussels and scollops and clean the beard.

Cook langoustine in stock for 2 minutes and peel the tail.

Grill the diamonds of salmon and trout on both sides for 1 minute, all the fish should be undercooked. Place all fish on a tray with a butter paper on top to keep moist.

Reduce stock and wine and add saffron, reducing by half. Add double cream and reduce to the right consistency. Add both caviars at last minute so the caviar does not cook and go hard. Flash fish under the salamander. Saute seaweed in butter and season. Place on the plate. Arrange fish around seaweed. Spoon the sauce around the seafood and serve.

Royal Terrace Hotel

Senior Chef – WAYNE BOSWORTH

LEMON FISH FLAN

--- Serves 20 ---

INGREDIENTS

pastry:
1½ lb plain flour.
12 oz butter.
¼ pint water.
3 lemon rinds.
salt.
filling:
2 lb haddock or whiting fillets skinned
and diced.
2 lb smoked haddock skinned and diced.
½ lb onions.
½ lb frozen sliced green beans.
4 eggs beaten.
½ pint milk.
salt and black pepper.

Preheat oven to 200°C, 400°F, Gas Mark 6. Make the pastry and line flan ring or dish. Mix the fish with the onion and green beans, place in the pastry base. Mix the egg, milk and seasonings, pour over the fish mixture. Bake for 35-40 minutes. Serve with an accompanying vegetable.

Note: pastry may be baked blind if required.

Hibs FC

CREAMY COD PIE

Archbishop of Canterbury

INGREDIENTS

1 lb cod.
1 lb smoked haddock.
³/₄ pint milk.
1½ oz butter.
1½ oz flour.
½ pint single cream.
½ lb sliced mushrooms.
mashed potato made with:
1 lb potatoes.
butter and milk to bind.
salt and pepper.
parsley to garnish.

Bake fish in milk in a buttered fireproof dish till cooked (about 15 minutes).

Make a white sauce with the butter, flour, milk strained off the fish and cream. Season.

Add mushrooms and flaked fish to the sauce. Simmer for 5 minutes, then spoon into fireproof dish. Cover with mashed potato, and bake in oven until potato is golden brown (about 20 minutes).

Sprinkle with parsley.

THE PAVILION
RESTAURANT & BAR

'Kevin O'Keefe has recently joined the hotel after various posts in international and exclusive country house restaurants. His arrival here coincides with the opening of the "Pavilion," a new restaurant based loosely on a Colonial theme.
In addition to the various speciality dishes perfected by Kevin and included in our a la carte menus, you can also enjoy a choice from our hot and cold buffet.
Prices are surprisingly lower than usually expected of an international hotel and this is because we are aiming our efforts at the local community and want them to return time and time again.'

Open for lunch from September onwards 12.30–2.00
(except Saturdays when closed) and dinner, in the evening, from 6.30.

HILTON NATIONAL
EDINBURGH

Belford Road, Edinburgh EH4 3DG. Tel. (031) 332 2545
Telex 727979 Fax. (031) 332 3805

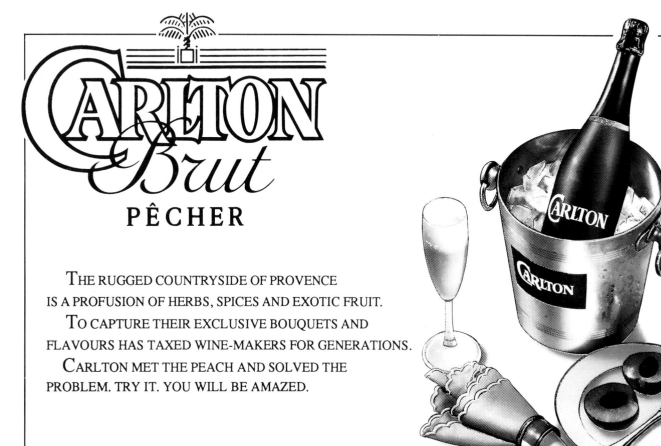

FISH CURRY

Sheena McDonald STV

—— Serves 20 ——

INGREDIENTS

4 oz low fat spread.
1 lb onions sliced.
3 oz curry powder.
3 oz flour.
1½ pints fish or chicken stock.
1 14 oz can tomatoes.
5 lb cod/coley fillets skinned and diced.
3 oz tomato puree.
8 oz apples chopped.
4 oz seedless raisins.
salt and pepper.
2½ lb brown rice.

Melt fat and cook onions and curry powder for 2-3 minutes. Add flour and cook for 1-2 minutes. Add stock gradually and mix well. Add tomatoes and bring to the boil. Add diced fish. Simmer fish for 5-6 minutes until just tender. Add remaining ingredients, warm-through and serve with brown rice.

FISH PIE

Stanley Baxter

INGREDIENTS

1 lb haddock.
4 oz shelled prawns.
1 oz butter.
1 oz flour.
3 generous tablespoons of parsley.
freshly ground black pepper.
sea salt.
approx ³/₄ pint milk.

Remove the skin from the haddock by placing it under a hot grill for a few minutes. Then cover it well with milk and poach for 20 minutes.

Melt the butter, add the flour then add milk from the haddock. Break the haddock into small pieces, add the prawns, parsley, pepper and salt.

FISH WELLINGTON

INGREDIENTS

4 oz (100 g) mushrooms (whipped and chopped).
1 oz (25 g) butter.
4 tablespoons fresh double cream (60 ml).
2 large fillets of cod, or haddock about 2 lb (900 g).
13 oz (368 g) packet puff pastry.
2 oz (50 g) finely chopped onions.
6 oz (175 g) smooth liver pate.
salt and freshly ground pepper.
beaten egg to glaze.

Fry chopped onions and mushrooms in the butter until soft. Remove pan from heat.

Mash liver pate in a bowl, stir in the cream, onions and mushrooms. Season to taste.

Remove skin from fish, roll out pastry to rectangle, 14 x 21" (35 x 30 cm). Place 1 fillet in the centre of the pastry, spread filling mixture over fillet then top with other fillet. Trim pastry round allowing a good 4" (10 cm) border. Reserve the trimmings. Brush round edges of pastry with beaten egg then carefully fold it over the fish and neatly wrap it up like a parcel.

Place the parcelled fish on a baking sheet with sealed edges down. Brush with beaten egg. Roll pastry trimmings into decoreture fish shapes, seal on top parcel. Bake at 425°F/220°C (Gas Mark 7), for 25 minutes until golden brown (until fish is cooked).

Faith Brown

HERRING AND YOGHURT SALAD

———— Serves 20 ————

INGREDIENTS

20 8 oz whole herrings.
1 lb medium onions sliced.
12 peppercorns.
1 pint tarragon vinegar.
2 pints fish stock for cooking.
1 pint natural yoghurt.
4 eating apples.
1 lemon's juice.

Preheat oven to 160°C, 325°F, Gas Mark 3.

Clean and bone the herrings. Roll the fish up from head to tail and secure with a cocktail stick. Place the fish in a shallow ovenproof dish and cover with the onion slices, seasonings and liquids. Poach in the oven for 30 minutes. Remove from the oven and chill.

When chilled, drain the fish reserving the liquid and arrange on a serving dish. Strain the liquid and blend a little of the strained liquid with the yoghurt. Pour over the fish and serve garnished with apple slices dipped in lemon juice.

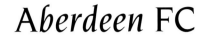

Aberdeen FC

ITALIAN FISH STEW

Dennis Law

—— Serves 20 ——

INGREDIENTS

2-3 fl oz sunflower oil.
3 onions sliced.
3 garlic cloves.
2½ lb carrots peeled and cut into strips.
5 lb cod/haddock fillets, skinned and cubed.
1 x A10 canned tomatoes.
10 black olives.
1 lb shelled mussels.
oregano to taste.
salt and black pepper.
parsley chopped.

Heat the oil and cook the vegetables for 2-3 minutes without browning. Add the fish, cover and cook for 5-6 minutes. Add the tomatoes, olives, mussels and seasonings and cook for another 2-4 minutes.

Serve garnished with chopped parsley.

BAKED PLAICE WITH ORANGES

——— Serves 20 ———

INGREDIENTS

2 14 oz cans mandarin oranges in natural juices.
2 lemons, juice and rind.
1/2 teaspoon cayenne pepper.
20 6 oz plaice fillets skinned.
4 oz polyunsaturated margarine.
salt and black pepper.
2 oz flaked almonds.
chopped parsley to garnish.

Preheat oven to 190°C, 375°F, Gas Mark 5.

Sprinkle oranges and grated lemon rind over base of a large greased oveproof dish. Season with cayenne pepper.

Season the fillets, skinned side up, with salt and pepper. Roll up and place on top of oranges. Sprinkle with lemon juice and dot with margarine.

Cover and bake for 20-25 minutes.

Serve sprinkled with almonds and parsley.

Hearts FC

LOBSTER THERMIDOR

David Gower

—— Serves 4 ——

INGREDIENTS

4 uncooked lobsters (split in half).
chopped shallots.
¼ pint white wine.
1 oz flour.
½ pint double cream.
1 egg yolk beaten.
fresh parsley.
tarragon.
parmesan cheese.
olive oil.
1 oz butter.
½ pint milk.
cayenne pepper.
French mustard.

Put the split lobsters (shell side down) under a low grill with a brushing of oil over them. Cook for about 15 minutes – till meat looks cooked.

In the meantime, bring to the boil the shallots, herbs and wine. Then reduce till only a couple of tablespoons of liquid left. Strain and set aside.

In another pan, melt the butter and stir in the flour. Then slowly add the milk and cream, stirring all the while. Add the cayenne pepper, and salt, if wanted, to taste. Add the reduced wine and cook till the sauce thickens. Then remove from the heat and stir in the egg yolk and mustard. Keep the sauce warm over warm water (a bain-marie), stirring frequently.

Now back to the lobsters. When cooked, move from the grill, putting up the heat. Remove the meat from the shells (and claws if cooked), and cut into cubes or chunks. Mix half the sauce in with the meat, and then replace in the shells. Pour the remaining sauce over the tops and coat with parmesan cheese. Grill till golden brown.

SALMON KEDGEREE

Betty Driver

—— Serves 5 ——

INGREDIENTS

1 cup raw long grain rice.
7 oz tin of red salmon
(or fresh if well off).
¼ cup of butter.
2 hard boiled eggs finely chopped.
3 tablespoons double cream.
freshly ground pepper.
pinch of cayenne pepper.
chopped parsley.

Cook rice in boiling water until tender, drain well and keep hot over boiling water. If using cooked fresh salmon, remove all skin and bones and flake gently, if tinned drain and flake.

Melt the butter in a pan, add the fish, eggs, cream, salt and peppers to taste and stir until hot. Combine this fish mixture with the hot rice and add the chopped parsley, turn onto hot serving dish and shape into a pyramid with fork.

Smoked cod can be substituted for the salmon, but add ½ an onion lightly fried.

SMOKED MACKEREL AND APPLE SALAD

--- Serves 20 ---

INGREDIENTS

4 lb "hot" smoked mackerel fillets skinned.
2 lb red or green apples cored and diced.
8 oz celery chopped.
4 oz raisins.
salt and black pepper.
lemon juice.
1/4 pint natural yoghurt.
2 lettuces.

Cut fillets into cubes. Mix in the apples, celery, raisins and season with salt, pepper and lemon juice. Add sufficient yoghurt to coat salad.

Serve on a bed of crisp lettuce.

Rangers FC

Because your eyes need to focus at different distances, reading glasses can become a tiresome inconvenience. As can constantly switching between two pairs of spectacles.

Which is why so many people peer over the top of their frames or end up with them on the end of their noses.

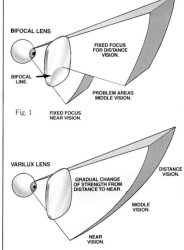

BIFOCAL LENS

FIXED FOCUS FOR DISTANCE VISION.

BIFOCAL LINE.

PROBLEM AREAS MIDDLE VISION.

Fig. 1   FIXED FOCUS NEAR VISION.

VARILUX LENS

GRADUAL CHANGE OF STRENGTH FROM DISTANCE TO NEAR.

DISTANCE VISION.

MIDDLE VISION.

NEAR VISION.

Bifocals are a practical solution, but they too have their limitations. Occasionally missing a step, reading prices through a shop window or working in the garden are problems which will

VARILUX LENS

BIFOCAL LENS

APPROXIMATE COMPARISON BETWEEN THE LENSES.

strike a chord with many bifocal wearers.

These problems can arise because the

DONT PUT UP WITH BI FOCALS WHEN YOU COULD PUT ON VARILUX LENSES

corrections in bifocals are fixed. The line between the two portions of the lens marks the jump your eye must make between near and distance vision and Fig. 1 illustrates the gap that can exist between the two.

As you grow older and your eyesight naturally worsens this 'no-man's-land' can grow until trifocals are needed to overcome the problem.

But through Varilux lenses that gap, and the wearying jump your eyes must make across it, disappears completely. Unlike bifocals, the correction in a Varilux lens changes gradually from distance vision at the top of the lens, through middle distance to near vision in the lower section. That smooth progression helps your eye to progress smoothly from near to distance vision. Your eye naturally finds the part of the lens it needs to see clearly at any distance.

And you will not only see better with Varilux you will look better too because there is no bifocal line. A line many bifocal wearers feel to be an unwelcome reminder of advancing years.

Varilux can be worn in a wide range of frames, including the fashionable larger sizes and are themselves available in a wide range of tints in both glass and plastic. They are available too with a unique reflection free coating which will make your lenses practically invisible. The result is clearer, brighter vision, better eye contact and an end to annoying ghost images.

All over the world 30 million

people are enjoying the benefits of Varilux lenses.

To find out if you are suitable for a Varilux prescription simply visit a qualified optician. You'll find Varilux the next best thing to perfect eyesight.

VISIBLY SUPERIOR VARILUX

TROTA SULLA BRACE (BARBECUED TROUT WITH GARLIC & ROSEMARY)

Linda Lusardi

─── Serves 4 ───

INGREDIENTS

2 garlic cloves peeled and crushed.
2 springs rosemary, divided into short lengths.
4 trout about 8 oz (225 g) each – cleaned.
6 tablespoons olive oil.
salt.
freshly ground black pepoer.
finely grated rind of $\frac{1}{2}$ lemon.
3 tablespoons lemon juice.
16 pitted green olives.
16 blanched almonds.

Mix together the garlic and rosemary and use to fill the body cavities of the trout. Lay the fish in a shallow dish.

Mix olive oil with salt and pepper to taste, add the lemon rind and juice, spoon evenly over the trout. Cover and chill for 3-4 hours.

Remove the trout from their marinade and drain, reserving the marinade. Place the fish on the greased grill of a pre-heated barbecue and grill for 6 minutes (you can use a fish clamp if you like). Brush the trout on both sides with the marinade and place them other side down on the barbecue. Grill for a further 6 minutes or until trout are tender.

Meanwhile press an almond into each green olive then roll the olives lightly in the remaining marinade.

Arrange the cooked trout on a serving dish and garnish with the almond stuffed olives (you can marinate for up to 24 hours if trout are fresh).

FINE SCOTTISH TROUT

Royal Terrace Hotel Edinburgh

Cold Smoking: – The same process used for smoking salmon is now popular for curing large pink Rainbow Trout (sometimes called "Salmon" Trout). The fish are split and the sides brined and then slowly smoked over cool oak chippings. The result is a truly luxurious product almost indistinguishable from finest smoked salmon, with a delicacy of flavour all its own. Very competitively priced, it is available from selected Trout Farms and wholesalers as whole sides or ready sliced and laid back for easy service. Serve traditionally with lemon, black pepper and brown bread and butter.

Whisky Trout:– Flour trout and saute in butter for 2 minutes each side. Add a splash of whisky to the pan and finish cooking, turning fish once. Remove to serving dish, boil up juices with a little cream and chopped parsley and pour over trout.

Herb Trout with Pernod:– Slash trout and moisten well with pernod or gin. Stuff cavity with fresh or dried fennel or dill and grill under medium heat, basting with pan juices. A simpler dish can be made using lemon juice and any available herbs like rosemary, parsley or tarragon.

Chef De Parti – ROY S. BRETT

The electric, gas, l.p.g. or solid fuel Aga comes in red, blue, green, brown, cream, black or white.

For further details write to: Aga, Freepost, P.O. Box 30, Ketley, Telford, Shropshire TF14 DD. Tel 0952 641100

 Aga. A member of the Glynwed International plc group of companies.

AGA

Meat

BEEF IN ORANGE SAUCE

Dame Denise Brett
DLJ MBE

INGREDIENTS

1½ lbs (675 g) Scotch round beef cubed.
salt and pepper.
2 teaspoons (10 ml) dried sage.
1 small onion finely chopped.
1 clove garlic finely chopped.
½ oz (912.5 g) cornflour.
½ pint (275 ml) stock beef.
4 fl oz (100 ml) fresh orange juice.
2 fresh oranges – segmented
(pith and skin removed).
1 fl oz (25 ml) cooking oil.
1 carrot sliced.
2 oz (50 g) button mushrooms sliced.
½ fl oz (15 ml) cointreau (optional).

Season the cubed meat with a pinch of salt and pepper and the sage. Heat oil and fry onion, mushrooms, carrot and garlic until softened. Brown meat on all sides, remove from pan and leave on one side. Stir cornflour into the remaining fat and cook for a few minutes. Gradually add stock and orange juice and bring to the boil. Return beef to pan reduce heat. Add orange segments to the sauce retaining a few for garnish. Cover and simmer for ½ hour add cointreau. Simmer for further ½ hour. Garnish with remaining orange segments and a little chopped parsley. Can be served with boiled rice or potatoes and green vegetables.

BEEF GOULASH AND NOODLES

Anna Wing

INGREDIENTS

2 lb lean beef (top rump).
3 tablespoons of Hungarian paprika.
4 large onions chopped.
small green pepper diced.
teaspoon salt.
1¹/₂ pints stock (or water).
2 tablespoons butter.

Melt the butter and add the onions. Saute until golden brown. Season beef with salt and pepper. Saute until brown. Add paprika and green pepper and mix into a paste. Put all the ingredients together.

Add stock (or water), bring to the boil and simmer for 2¹/₂ hours until the meat falls apart. Place the whole on the top of 1 lb of noodles which have been boiled in 1 pint of water for 20 minutes.

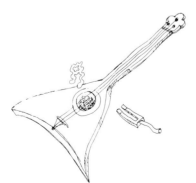

BEEF SATAY

Ruth Madoc

INGREDIENTS

1½ lbs lean beef (sirloin or rump).
1 tablespoon blanched almonds.
1 tablespoon sliced root ginger.
1 level teaspoon ground coriander.
1 level teaspoon turmeric.
½ pint coconut milk.
salt, black pepper.
1 level teaspoon brown sugar to taste.
sauce:
2 onions.
1-2 tablespoons peanut oil.
3 oz roasted peanuts.
½ level teaspoon chilli powder.
1 level teaspoon light brown sugar.
salt to taste.
1 tablespoon soya sauce.
juice of half of a lime.

Pound almonds, ginger, coriander and turmeric to a paste in a mortar and gradually dilute it with coconut milk.

Cut the meat into bite size pieces and sprinkle them with salt and pepper. Marinate the meat in the spiced coconut milk for 2 hours.

Remove meat from marinate and thread on to one end of a skewer, sprinkle them with sugar and grill, turning and basting frequently with marinate. Allow 2 skewers per person and serve with satay sauce.

Sauce:
Peel and thinly slice 1 onion and fry in the hot peanut oil. Peel and finely chop the second onion and pound it with the peanuts and chilli powder in a mortar or liquidiser.

Add this paste to the pan and fry for a further 3 minutes, stirring continuously. Gradually dilute the mixture with ¼ pint warm water and stir in the sugar. Cook for a few minutes until the sauce has the consistency of single cream. Season to taste with salt, soya sauce and lime juice.

Serve the sauce hot.

BITOKES A LA RUSSE

Hamburgers with cream sauce.

INGREDIENTS

1½ lb lean minced beef.
3 oz finely chopped onions.
1 oz softened butter, ground beef suet or fresh pork fat.
1½ teaspoons salt.
⅛ teaspoon pepper.
⅛ teaspoon thyme.
1 egg.

Add beef, butter or fat, seasonings and egg to the onions in a mixing bowl and heat vigorously to blend thoroughly. Correct seasoning. Form into patties ¾″ thick. Take ½ oz butter and 1 dessert spoon of oil, or enough to fill bottom of frying pan. Cook over moderate heat. Remove to hot serving dish.

Take:
⅛ pint stock or beef bouillon.
¼ pint cream.
salt and pepper.
pinch of nutmeg.
drops of lemon juice.

Pour the fat out of the frying pan. Add the stock or bouillon and boil it down rapidly, scraping up coagulates cooking juices until reduced almost to a syrup. Pour in cream and boil it down rapidly for a minute or two until it has been reduced and thickened slightly. Season to taste with salt, pepper, nutmeg and drops of lemon juice.

Take:
1-1½ oz softened butter.
2 tablespoons chopped green herbs, such as parsley, chives, tarragon, chevril OR parsley only.

Remove the frying pan away from the heat, swirl in the butter by dessert spoon until it is absorbed. Stir in the herbs, spoon the sauce over the hamburgers and serve.

Ronnie Corbett

"My lifelong love of song and poetry sprang from my very Scottish upbringing. The poet Burns was often on my father's lips, and I could see that my father shared with the Immortal Bard the same whole-hearted enjoyment of life, love of people, sympathy with sinners, and distance from the self-righteous. And once a year – at table on Hogmanay – we said Rabbie's Grace:

Some hae meat and canna eat,
Some wad eat but want it.
But we hae meat, and we can eat,
So let the Lord be thankit . . .

We said it seriously, because we were taught to mean it. I could never forget those magical meals, over fifty years ago in Liverpool. We were tightly bound together in intimacy. At the same time what we were saying and doing reached back into the past, and offered such rich promise for the future."

BRAISED VEAL KNUCKLES WITH ORANGE SAUCE AND MASHED POTATOES

Savoy Grill

Chef – ALAN HILL

——— Serves 4 ———

INGREDIENTS

8 x 100 g veal knuckles.
salt and freshly ground pepper.
2 cl oil.
30 g butter.
60 g mirepoix.
30 g tomato paste.
10 cl white wine.
1 large orange, juice and zest.
1 large lemon, juice and zest.
30 cl veal gravy.
60 g brunoise of vegetables.
15 g chopped chives.
30 g butter to finish.

Season and seal the veal knuckles in a little hot oil and butter. Remove dry and keep warm.

Roast the mirepoix in the frying pan reaching a golden colour, remove dry and place upon the veal knuckles. Place the veal knuckles in a braising pan and deglace the frying pan with the white wine. Add the tomato puree and juice of the orange and lemon and bind together. Place the veal gravy into the mixture and pour over the knuckles, braise for two hours. When cooked remove from the sauce and place upon the serving dish.

Saute the brunoise of vegetables in a little butter along with the zest. Pass the sauce through a fine strainer and mount with butter. Check the seasoning and pour over the veal knuckles.

Garnish with the brunoise of vegetables and chopped chives. Serve mashed potatoes apart and serve immediately.

CHILI CON CARNE

Steve Cram

— Serve hot —

INGREDIENTS

1 lb minced beef.
1 large can plum tomatoes.
1 large can kidney beans.
1 large can baked beans.
¼ pint beef stock.
dash Worcestershire sauce.
1 clove garlic.
2 medium sized onions.
2 tablespoons tomato puree.
1 tablespoon olive oil.
salt and freshly ground pepper.
1½ teaspoons hot chili powder.
1 teaspoon mixed herbs.
1 bayleaf.

Slice onion, season with pepper and crushed garlic, fry in olive oil until soft. Add mince, fry until well browned. Add drained kidney beans, beef stock and bayleaf. Stir and add tomato puree and tomatoes. Stir and add baked beans and mixed herbs. Season with pepper, chili powder and Worcestershire sauce. Simmer for at least one hour.

Serve on jacket potatoes, rice or on its own with garlic bread.

JOHNNY CASH'S "OLD IRON POT" FAMILY STYLE CHILLI

Johnny Cash

—————— Serves 12 ——————

INGREDIENTS

5 lb sirloin steak.
*3 packages McCormicks, Schilling, Lawry's or any good chilli seasoning mix.
*Mexene chilli powder.
*Spice Island chilli con carne seasoning.
*cumin.
*thyme.
*sage leaves.
*chopped raw onions.
*chopped chilli peppers.
3 or 4 cans red kidney beans.
3 or 4 cans whole tomatoes.
1 can tomato paste.
*garlic powder.
*onion powder.
2 tablespoons sugar.
salt to taste.

Chop steak and cook until medium with a little shortening added. Add packages of chilli seasoning mix and cook for 5 minutes. Add beans, tomatoes, spices, raw onions, sugar and chilli powder and/or chilli con carne mix. Taste. If chilli is too hot for the children or ladies, add 1 or 2 cans of tomatoes. Add tomato paste. If it gets too thick, add water. Simmer low for 20 minutes. Serve with soda crackers and Pepsi or Coke. This will serve 12 people (3 helpings each).

*You must guess at the amount to use. I do not measure them.

NOTE (from John): Johnny Cash's "Old Iron Pot" Family Style Chilli will be better tomorrow than today if properly taken care of overnight!

"This recipe has never been given to anyone. Many people have asked for it, but I have never given them the true ingredients. (I have been known to substitute things like snake meat and such for the steak). When my mother asked me for the recipe for her book, I finally consented, and I guarantee that this is the recipe I use."

THE LENNY HENRY KILLER CHILLI

— Serves 4 —

Lenny Henry

INGREDIENTS

1 lb minced beef.
2 big onions.
2 green peppers.
tin Italian tomatoes.
tin kidney beans.
chilli powder (mild or hot dependent on whether your tongue is made of leather).
pinch oregano.
pinch mixed spices.
pinch cloves.
dash tabasco.
glass of red wine.
2 beef oxo cubes.
¼ lb mushrooms.
lucky rabbit's foot.

Yum yum in my tum.

Place rabbit's foot round your neck (you're going to need all the luck you can get because I certainly don't know what I'm doing).

Chop onions and green peppers. Fry in about 4 oz butter until they are fairly transluscent (that means see-through, thicky) add the meat and fry until it is bubbling noisily. Add tomato puree, about 1 tablespoon and stir until sauce thickens. Add all the spices and herbs, chop mushrooms, add them and stir for brown. Add tomatoes and stir for a couple of minutes until it is bubbling noisily. Add tomato puree, about 1 table-spoon and stir until sauce thickens. Add all the spices and herbs, chop mushrooms, add them and stir for two minutes. Add kidney beans and give it a good stir. Add dash of tabasco and crumble in Oxo cubes and glass of wine and stir again. Put on low heat (eg Gas Mark 2) and simmer for about one hour stirring occasionally. After this time it should be a lovely dark brown colour and quite thick. If there is a layer of fat on top, scrape off with a spoon.
Serve with rice or pitta bread to about 4 people.

FILLET STEAK BALMORAL

INGREDIENTS

1 8 oz fillet steak.
½ pint single cream.
1 measure Scotch whisky.
4 oz mushrooms cooked and pureed.

Grill steak to taste. Mix cream and whisky to make sauce. Spread mushroom puree over steak and pour over sauce.

ESCALOPE OF VENISON WITH WILD RASPBERRY SAUCE

Serves 2

INGREDIENTS

8 oz venison loin.
¼ lb wild raspberries (or ordinary raspberries).
2 oz butter.
1 small glass of port.
pinch of sugar.
2 oz double cream.
salt and pepper.
fresh mint leaves.

Cut four 2 oz portions of venison from the 8 oz piece. Bat out gently with a rolling pin and saute them in the 2 oz of butter until cooked (do not saute them too hard as they will shrink). Remove from butter and put to one side. Add the port and bring to the boil. Puree the raspberries and add to the port, allow the sauce to reduce by half, season with the sugar, salt and pepper.

Arrange the venison in an appropriate dish and cover with the sauce. Pour the cream over the top and around the edges of the venison, garnish with mint leaves and serve.

Andy Cameron

Capital Hotel, Edinburgh

Head Chef – DOUGLAS MACDONALD
Senior Sous Chef – BREMNER MACDONALD

The Dalhousie Castle Hotel

****
AA Four Star

Bonnyrigg
Edinburgh
EH19 3JB
Tel: (0875) 20153

72% Egon Ronay

Ideally situated in acres of Parkland yet only 8 miles from Edinburgh, this 4 star hotel practises the finest traditions of Scottish hospitality.

Dalhousie Castle has been host to Monarchs and Noblemen for 8 long centuries and today offers 25 individually designed bedchambers all with en-suite bathroom, colour T.V., radio and direct dial telephone. Both guests and non-residents are invited to the Library Bar before dining in the unique Dungeon Dining Room which has gained international acclaim for its fine cuisine.

The romantic setting adds the fairytale touches to any wedding function, whilst the Conference organiser can choose a venue from the numerous Meeting Rooms.

For further details and reservations
Telephone 0875 20153

THE LUNDIN LINKS

H O T E L
LUNDIN LINKS
FIFE KY8 6AP
S C O T L A N D
TELEPHONE 0333 320207
FAX 0333 320930

Welcome to a golfer's Paradise with 35 courses within 25 miles including St. Andrews.

Enjoy a golfing holiday from as little as £29.50 per person per day (weekly rate), incl. Dinner, Bed and Breakfast with free golf on Lundin Links (qualifying course for the Open) or the unique 'Course-A-Day' golf break for two, three, four or more days.

All rooms have en-suite bath/shower, colour T.V., telephone and tea/coffee making facilities.

My chef and friendly staff will make your stay a memorable one.

Resident Proprietor:– David Tong.
Telephone or write for details.

BANDRUM NURSING HOME

A Caring and Relaxed Atmosphere Combined with 24-hour Trained Staff Cover

A private nursing home set in 18 acres of woodland and garden providing the highest standards of nursing care.
23 beds, increasing to 39 after completion of work and further registration.

We offer:–
- Occupational Therapy Dept. (tailored to the individual needs of each patient)
- Physiotherapy
- Good home cooking
- Provision for special diets
- Breakfast in bed, optional
- Laundry service
- Comfortable lounges with colour T.V.

- Heat and smoke detectors installed
- Full central heating
- Telephone facilities in every room
- Nurse call system
- Colour T.V. facilities in every room
- Hairdressing
- Chiropody

Saline Near Dunfermline ● Telephone 851030

BRIDGEND HOTEL
HIGH STREET
KINROSS   KY13 7EN
TELEPHONE: 0577 63413
FAX NO: 0577 64769

Bridgend Hotel, situated in High Street, Kinross, Tayside. Just one mile from Junction 6 on the M90.

Our newly refurbished "Poachers Bar and Restaurant" provides lunches and suppers seven days per week. Coach parties catered for, by arrangement.

Weddings, Dinner Dance and Conference facilities are available. The Mary Stuart Suite can accommodate up to 250 guests.

A 12 bedroomed Hotel, we are ideally situated for day trips to both Perth and Edinburgh and just a few minutes walk from historic, picturesque Loch Leven. Famous for its trout fishing and of course, Castle Island where the ruins of Loch Leven Castle bring memories of the daring escape of Mary, Queen of Scots.

HAGGIS

Gordon Honeycombe

Here is my favourite 'Haggis' recipe. I thought it appropriate as I'm ³/₄ Scottish and was educated in Edinburgh. I love eating Haggis with 'neaps' and a dram.

It's from the notebook of the Hon. Mrs. Hay Mackenzie of Cromarty.

INGREDIENTS

a mutton paunch.
the heart, lungs and liver of a sheep.
salt.
white and cayenne pepper.
nutmeg.
onions.
oatmeal (a handful).
1 lb beef suet.
1 glass strong stock.
old whisky or Athole brose (mixture of equal parts of whisky, cream and honey).
time to boil: ¹/₂ hour at first,
then 3 hours.

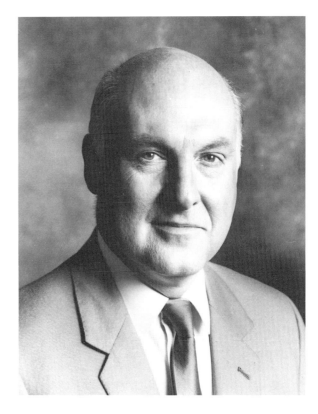

Wash the paunch and turn it inside out. Boil the heart, lungs and liver together for half an hour. Chop the meat very finely except half the liver, which must be grated when quite cold.

Spread the chopped mixture on a table and season with the salt, pepper and nutmeg. Chop the onions. Add the grated liver and a handful of oatmeal. Chop the suet and add that. Mix all well together with the stock. Fill the paunch, leaving plenty of room for the oatmeal to swell. Sew it up. Prick it all over with a needle. Boil for 3 hours.

Serve with old whisky or Athole brose.

This is also Mrs. MacIver's recipe (Edinburgh 1773) but she adds: 'Be sure to put out all the wind before you sew up the bag.' Mrs. MacIver was the daughter of a Highland laird impoverished through supporting Bonnie Prince Charlie. His daughter, a first-rate cook, turned her genius to account by setting up as a cookery teacher in Edinburgh. Her book, the property of one of her descendants (Mrs. MacIver Cruickshank of Nairn) would delight Mr. Morton Shand who regrets the substitution in Scotland of the term 'butcher' for the old Scottish word 'flesher'; Mrs. MacIver classifies all her meat receipts under the heading 'Flesh.'

JERSEY BEAN CROCK

This is a traditional Channel Island dish.

INGREDIENTS

2 lb mixed dried beans.
1 hock or 2 trotters.
2 lbs belly pork.
1 large onion.
a little pepper and salt.

Soak beans overnight. Place ingredients in large pot or casserole. Add plenty of water. Place in oven for 12 hours.

Remove fat and bone from meat. Season. A little dry cider may be added.

HOT POT

— Serves 6-8 —

INGREDIENTS

1 lb beef chuck steak (cut into 1" pieces).
1 gill water.
6 medium potatoes peeled and sliced.
4 medium onions peeled and sliced.
6 carrots peeled and sliced.
3 teaspoons salt.
1 x 1 lb can tomatoes.
$^1/_2$ teaspoon tabasco.

Sprinkle beef with salt, brown thoroughly in a small amount of fat. Remove beef. add water to fat in pan. Cook, stirring constantly to blend bits of meat left in pan. Remove from heat.

Layer beef, potatoes, onions and carrots in casserole, sprinkling each layer with salt and a little tabasco, and adding tomatoes on each layer. Pour water and fat over (top layer being potato).

Cook in medium oven for at least 2 hours at 350-360°F.

Wendy Richard

"My most memorable meal is the first time my now fiance took me to supper. I don't recall what I ate, but I was so nervous I put my elbow in the butter! Paul moved the dish to the other side of the table – I stubbed my cigarette in it! He said "I thought I was the one who is Irish.""

Cyril Smith MBE, MP

KASHMIRI-STYLE LAMB

My current favourite lamb dish which gets rave reviews (so far). I know it looks difficult but I have found that I keep the spices together in a small box so that they are all on hand and the fiddle really is worthwhile as it is a very unique taste.

INGREDIENTS

3 lb leg of lamb.
1 level tablespoon poppy seeds.
3 level tablespoon grated fresh or desiccated coconut.
2 medium onions, skinned and coarsely chopped.
2" piece root ginger, peeled and coarsely chopped.
1 oz blanched almonds chopped.
cinnamon stick (2" long).
6 green cardamoms.
3 black cardamoms ground.
4 cloves.
small piece of mace.
$\frac{1}{2}$ level teaspoon grated nutmeg.
$1\frac{1}{2}$ level teaspoons mild chilli powder.
1 level teaspoon salt.
5 fl oz natural yoghurt.
5 oz ghee or butter, melted.
4 bayleaves crushed.
2 level tablespoons ground aniseed.

Remove some fat from the leg of lamb. Prick the meat all over with a sharp knife. Place in a deep baking dish or a roasting tin.

Soak the poppy seeds and the coconut in a little warm water for 10 minutes. Drain and put in a blender or food processor with the next 11 ingredients and blend to a smooth paste.

Pour the paste over the meat and spread all over, coating well and making sure the mixture penetrates into the cuts.

Mix together the yoghurt and remaining ingredients and spread it over the lamb. Cook in the oven at 170°C (Gas Mark 3) for $2\frac{1}{4}$-$2\frac{1}{2}$ hours, basting frequently. Remove from the oven and transfer to a warmed serving dish.

Vince Hill

ORIENTAL LAMB

——— Serves 4 ———

INGREDIENTS

1 lb (500 g) leg of Scotch lamb, cut into
1½" strips.
6 large firm tomatoes or 1 medium tin of
chopped tomatoes.
4 tablespoons (60 ml) olive oil.
2 garlic cloves finely chopped.
freshly ground black pepper.
salt.
6 tablespoons (90 ml) spring onions
thinly sliced.
6 tablespoons (90 ml) finely chopped
parsley.
grated rind of 1 lemon.
5 oz (125 g) bean sprouts (can be stirred
into mixture or lightly sauted and used
as a base).
garnish:
3 spring onions (1 finely chopped).
½ small red pepper finely chopped.
selection of nuts.

Lower the tomatoes into boiling water
for about 30 seconds then remove them
with a slotted spoon, skin them at once
and cut them into quarters.

Heat the olive oil in a large thick
bottomed frying pan. Add the lamb strips
and cook over a high heat until well
browned on all sides. Season generously
with salt ad freshly ground pepper and
stir in half of the finely chopped garlic.
Add the tomato strips and continue to
cook stirring continuously for about
3 minutes.

Add the thinly sliced spring onions, bean
sprouts and finely chopped parsley. Toss
well over the heat then sprinkle with the
grated lemon rind and the remaining
finely chopped garlic. Cover the pan and
allow the aromatics to heat through for
10 minutes before serving.

Garnish and serve.

Loon Fung Restaurant Edinburgh

LANCASHIRE HOT POT

Cecil Parkinson

—— Serves 6 ——

INGREDIENTS

2 lb best end of neck.
2 large onions.
4 large potatoes.
1 beef stock.
seasoning.
water (with beef stock)

Brown meat in frying pan.

Chop up onions, peel and slice potatoes.

When meat is browned, place layer of meat in the bottom of a heavy casserole dish, then a layer of onions, then a layer of potatoes. Add beef stock and water. Finish with layer of potato, completely covering top.

Simmer for 2 hours.

Before serving, place under hot grill to brown and crisp top layer of potatoes.

← BLUE HOT!

LIVER HOT POT

This is my favourite, but my wife Di's recipe. I hope you understand it better than I do.

INGREDIENTS

1 lb lambs liver – thinly sliced.
1 oz plane flour (from your local airport Duty Free Shop) or any other kind of flour. Is that plain?
salt and freshly ground black pepper.
1 oz butter (you could use margarine, but a bitta butter's better).
4 rashers of streaky bacon, rinded and chopped.
2 large onions, peeled and sliced (to avoid tears, wear a snorkle and mask).
½ pint beef stock.
2 teaspoons tomato ketchup (use same spoon twice).
½ teaspoon dried mixed herbs (cut spoon in half?).
1 tablespoon finely chopped parsley (chop the parsley, not the spoon).

Toss liver in the flour (try not to miss), seasoned with salt and pepper. Reserve any left over flour.

Heat the butter in a pan, add liver and fry briskly in the fat for 2 minutes, then transfer to shallow dish.

Add bacon and onion to pan and fry until golden brown. Sprinkle in any left over flour and cook for 1 minute, stirring constantly. Gradually stir in the stock, ketchup and mixed herbs and bring to the boil, stirring constantly. (Stirring stuff, isn't it?). Remove from the heat and stir in parsley, taste and adjust seasoning and pour sauce over liver.

Cover the container and bake in a moderate oven, 350°F (Gas Mark 4), for 20 minutes.

Serve (underhand) with mashed potatoes, carrots and green cabbage.

Johnny Ball

NB: the dish can be frozen after cooking (and so can the liver) – cool, cover, seal and freeze.

To serve – re-heat covered in moderate oven for about 50 minutes or until heated through.

MEAT PIE CANNON

Cheap, filling and tasty pie with a layer of sliced potatoes in the middle.

——————— Serves 4 ———————

INGREDIENTS

1 large onion peeled and sliced.
4 carrots, peeled and diced.
4 sticks celery, chopped.
1 turnip, peeled and diced.
3 tablespoons oil.
1½ lb (700 g) stewing steak, trimmed and cubed.
½ pint (300 ml) beef stock.
1 bayleaf.
salt and pepper.
1 lb (450 g) potatoes, peeled, thickly sliced and boiled.
13 oz (375 g) packet puff pastry.
1 egg beaten.

Fry onions, carrots, celery and turnip in oil for a few minutes. Add meat and fry until browned. Pour over stock, add bayleaf, salt and pepper. Bring to the boil and simmer for 2 hours, stirring occasionally. Allow to cool. Place half the meat mixture in a pie dish. Add a layer of potatoes. Pour remaining mixture on top. Roll out pastry on a lightly floured top. Cut strip of pastry to cover rim of dish and dampen. Lay pastry on top, seal and trim. Pinch edges together. Pierce pastry top with thre holes, using a skewer. Glaze with beaten egg. Cook at 400°F/200°C (Gas Mark 6), for 30 minutes or until well risen and golden brown.

Cannon & Ball

BOBBY'S LOBBY

A tasty meat and potato hash from Bobby's home village.

——————— Serves 4 ———————

INGREDIENTS

1 onion, peeled and chopped.
1 oz (25 g) butter.
1½ lb (700 g) minced beef.
1½ lb (700 g) potatoes, peeled and diced.
dash of Worcestershire sauce.
salt and pepper.

Fry onion in butter until soft. Add mince and fry until browned. Add potatoes, sauce, salt and pepper. Cook for 30 minutes, stirring occasionally.

PICCATA OF VEAL

Nancy Reagan

———— Serves 6 ————

INGREDIENTS

12 trimmed, thin slices of veal.
$\frac{1}{2}$ cup flour.
2 eggs beaten in a small bowl.
1 tablespoon chopped parsley.
$\frac{1}{4}$ cup grated romano cheese (optional).
$\frac{1}{2}$ cup vegetable oil.
salt and ground white pepper.

Slowly heat the oil in a large teflon pan or iron skillet. Sprinkle veal on both sides with salt and pepper. Then dip each veal slice very lightly on both sides in the flour. Mix together the parsley and the beaten eggs. Put the veal into the egg mixture, turning each slice. Sauté egg coated veal in the hot oil to a golden brown on both sides. Remove to a serving platter. Serve Veal Piccata with pasta or rice and tomatoes.

PORK PARCELS

INGREDIENTS

4 pork fillet steaks.
4 slices smoked ham.
4 slices mature cheddar cheese.
1 egg (beaten).
1 oz seasoned flour.
small packet breadcrumbs.

Slice through edge of pork fillets to form a pocket. Place one slice of ham and one slice of cheese into each pocket. Coat with seasoned flour, dip in egg and then breadcrumbs. Shallow fry over medium heat for approximately 8-10 minutes each side, or until cooked.

Gary Wilmot

"One of my favourite meals came about a few years ago. Having made some lovely friends in Summer Season in Colwyn Bay and knowing we would all be working in different parts of the country at Christmas time, our local restaurant, 'Blodwyns,' made us a full Christmas dinner – turkey, Christmas pud, mince pies – the works; they even decorated the restaurant with Christmas decorations! Santa Claus paid us a visit and all this on a lovely summer's evening in late August!"

THE CRAFTY COOK'S STEAK IN CREAM AND MUSTARD SAUCE

—— For each serving ——

INGREDIENTS

1 6 oz sirloin steak.
2 tablespoons double cream.
1 level dessert spoon grainy
french mustard.
½ oz butter per steak.

Melt the butter in frying pan. On high heat, sear steak for 30 seconds on each side. Turn heat lower and cook for 4 minutes. Pour on the cream and stir. Remove the steak, add the mustard to the cream and bring to the boil.

Season the steak and pour the sauce over.

SOUP N' STOVIES

INGREDIENTS

2½ lb potatoes.
2 large onions, chapped.
leftover roast meat, cut into large
chunks.
meat, dripping.
salt and pepper.

Peel potatoes and boil in salted water with the onions till they are tender. Drain off the water, and the liquid can be used for making soup, but back to the stovies, dry the potatoes well and then add the meat and dripping, break up the potatoes with a wooden spoon and mix well, then season and then you are ready to serve.

Michael Barry

Bob Malcolm

POT MESS

An unattractive name for a delicious time and money saving soup concocted on the mess decks of Her Majesty's larger ships.

Every month, just before the victualling allowance is credited to each mess, it is the practice to clear out every paticle of food left over from the previous month.

—— Serves as many as you like ——

To do this, every scrap and tin of edible left over food is piled willy-nilly into a large pot and heated through.

Sounds awful – tastes wonderful.

It's best to start with tinned soup as a base into which you can put any kind of meat or poultry – beef, pork, spam, corned beef etc., diced up and chucked in beside tinned peas, baked beans, tomatoes etc. Amazingly, the flavour is nearly always the same – ABSOLUTELY DELICIOUS.

It's great for small informal parties – or big ones if you have a lot of left overs! – or those supper breaks at the end of Trivial Pursuits.

Ricki Fulton

QUEUES DE BOEUF ENRUBANNEES A L'ECHALOTE

(Oxtail beribboned with vegetables and shallots)

——————— Serves 8 ———————

INGREDIENTS

5 lb 2 oz (2.4 kg) large oxtails.
1 lb 12 oz (700 g) large onions.
5 oz (150 g) celery.
2 lb 2 oz (1 kg) medium carrots.
2 dried orange peels (optional).
3 cloves.
1 tablespoon black peppercorns, crushed.
1 medium bouquet garni.
8 large button mushrooms, tightly closed.
2½ oz (70 g) garlic cloves.
3½ pts (2 L) red wine, preferably
Burgundy-style.
8 fl oz (200 ml) olive oil.
2 tablespoons flour.
1 pt (500 ml) veal stock.
2 or 3 pieces of pork rind (optional).
40 medium shallots.
7 oz (200 g) coarse salt.
10 oz (300 g) medium courgettes.
4 oz (100 g) butter.
parsley sprigs, to garnish.
fine salt.

Although this dish takes a long time to prepare, it is actually very simple to make. The combination of the different vegetables mingled with the oxtail gives a very pretty ribbon effect. It may be prepared and cooked up to 2 days in advance. When you want to serve the oxtail, reheat the meat in the strained cooking liquid, beat in the butter, a little at a time, then add the vegetable garnish.

The Day Before: Soak the oxtails in cold water for several hours. Drain and, using a sharp knife, cut off any excess fat if necessary. Cut the oxtails at each joint and place in an earthenware or pottery bowl. The Marinade: Peel and wash the onions, one-third of the carrots and the celery. Cut into large dice. Mix them into the oxtails, together with the orange peel, cloves, crushed peppercorns, bouquet garni and the unpeeled garlic. Remove the mushroom stalks, wash and stir into the oxtails. Reserve the mushroom caps.

Pour over the red wine and 4 tablespoons olive oil. Cover with greaseproof paper and leave to marinate in the refrigerator for 24 hours.

Preheat the oven to 190°C/375°F/Gas 5. Drain all the marinade ingredients in a large colander, set over a saucepan so as to catch the wine. Set the pan over high heat and boil the wine for several minutes. Keep warm. Pat the oxtail pieces dry with a cloth and salt lightly. Heat 4 tablespoons olive oil in a cocotte, casserole or Dutch oven set over high heat. Put in all the vegetables and aromatics from the marinade and brown for 6 to 8 minutes, stirring occasionally.

Heat the remaining olive oil in a sauté pan set over high heat, put in the oxtail pieces and brown them quickly on all sides. Lay them on the bed of vegetables and aromatics in the casserole. Sprinkle the flour onto a baking tray and roast in the hot oven until it is nutty brown. Sprinkle it over the oxtail at once and stir in with a wooden spatula.

Pour the wine from the marinade and the veal stock over the oxtail. Add about 1¾ pts (1 L) water; all the ingredients should be well covered with liquid. Lay the pork rind on top and bring to boil. Cover the casserole very tightly. Cook in the oven for 2½ hours.

Preparing The Vegetable Garnish: Increase the oven temperature to 200°C/400°F/Gas 6.

The Shallots: Arrange the unpeeled shallots on a bed of coarse salt in a roasting pan, making sure that they are not touching. Place in the preheated oven for about 14 minutes.

When the shallots are tender (check with

the point of a knife), remove from the oven, peel and keep at room temperature.

The Carrots: Peel and cut lengthways into slices $\frac{1}{10}$ in (3 mm) thick. Bring a pan of salted water to the boil, put in the carrots and cook for 3 minutes. Refresh, drain and lay the carrots on a tea-towel.

The Courgettes: Cut off the ends and cut the courgettes lengthways into slices $\frac{1}{10}$ in (3 mm) thick. Cook in boiling, salted water for 30 seconds, refresh in cold water, drain and lay them on the tea-towel with the carrots.

The Mushroom Caps: Wash them and cut slantways into slices $\frac{1}{10}$ in (3 mm) thick. Put them with the carrots and courgettes.

When the oxtail is cooked, carefully lift the pieces out of the casserole with a slotted spoon and put them in a deep serving dish. Cover with foil or a lid and keep warm.

Strain the liquid first through a colander and then through a sieve into a shallow pan. Set the pan over high heat and reduce the liquid by two-thirds, skimming the surface as often as necessary. The liquid should be slightly syrupy. Incorporate the butter, a little at a time.

Add the vegetable garnish and correct the seasoning with salt and pepper. As soon as the sauce comes to the boil, pour it over the oxtail. Sprinkle with finely chopped parsley and serve at once.

Michel Roux

STEAK DIANE

Gloria Hunniford

The secret of a good Steak Diane which I was given by a well known chef is as follows:

INGREDIENTS

fillet or rump steak.
onions.
mushrooms.
garlic.
Lea and Perrins sauce.
dry mustard.
brandy.
cream (double).
butter.

Batter the steaks until they are thin.

Coat the fillets or rump steak in dry mustard, then fry in butter. Remove the fillets from the pan and keep warm.

Add to the juices left in the pan: a finely chopped onion or onions, mushrooms, garlic, salt and pepper. When cooked add the Lea and Perrins, brandy and finally the cream – double cream preferably. Pour over fillets and serve with suitable green vegetables and potatoes.

NOTE: you don't <u>have to</u> flambé this recipe.

STEAK AND KIDNEY PIE

Kenny Lynch

My recipe is Steak and Kidney Pie. I can't tell you any particular meal I make it for, but I always do it for some girl I think is a darling and that happens quite a lot I'm pleased to say.

INGREDIENTS

1½ lb fillet steak.
4 oz Ox kidney.
salt and pepper.
1 tablespoon flour.
2 oz butter.
1 onion.
1 Oxo cube and 1 pint water.
Worcester sauce.
6 oz mushrooms.
pastry as you like it.

All My love
Kenny Lynch
xx

STEAK AND KIDNEY PIE

——— Serves 6 ———

INGREDIENTS

1$\frac{1}{2}$ lb stewing steak.
1 medium onion sliced.
1-1$\frac{1}{2}$ pints stock.
2 tablespoons tomato puree.
12 oz puff pastry.
$\frac{1}{2}$ lb kidney.
$\frac{1}{4}$ lb sliced mushrooms.
herbs – parsley and basil.
1 gill red wine.

Make the puff pastry. Cut the steak into cubes and cut up the kidney, removing the core. Put some oil or dripping in a fire proof dish and then fry the meat, add the onion and fry. Sprinkle 2 heaped tablespoons of flour over the meat and onion, put into a hot oven with the top off for 5 minutes, allowing the flour to soak up the fat. Then mix the flour in with the tomato puree. Add the stock, wine, mushrooms, chopped parsley and a large pinch of sweet basil. Bring to the boil and simmer for 1 hour. Adjust seasoning, put into a pie dish.

Roll out the pastry, put a strip of pastry round the edge of the dish, brush with water, put the pastry on top. Cut the sides with a knife and decorate the top with leaves made from the pastry trimmings. Brush with egg and put into a hot oven (375°-400°) for 30-35 minutes.

Rt Hon Michael Heseltine MP

STEAK AND KIDNEY PUD

Russell Grant

— Serves 4 —

INGREDIENTS

suet crust:
8 oz (225 g) plain flour.
4 oz (100 g) shredded suet.
salt.
cold water.
filling:
1 lb (450 g) chuck steak cubed.
4 oz (100 g) ox kidney cut up.
seasoned flour.
dripping (beef for preference) for frying.
2 onions.
gravy:
2 beef cubes.
1 teaspoon each of Worcestershire sauce
and marmite. Make up to a pint (600 ml)
with hot water.

To make suet pastry, mix flour, suet and little salt and add enough cold water to make a dough. Allow to rest before rolling out.

Roll the steak and kidney in seasoned flour and gently fry in beef dripping to seal in flavour. Fry the onions for about a minute.

Roll out pastry and line a 2 pint (1 litre) size basin, leaving enough pastry to make a lid. Put in steak, kidney and onions and pour in gravy, but not enough to fill the basin. Put on the pastry lid and seal the edges well. Cover with greaseproof paper and kitchen foil and steam for 4-5 hours.

Serve with mashed spuds and cabbage.

"I predict that this dish will go down great with your guests. It is one of my favourite dishes and not only is it good old English fare, but is quick and easy to make. However, if you are in a hurry to eat, be prepared for a long wait: it takes some hours to cook to perfection.

When eating alone, I make a smaller pudding by making up half the quantities, omitting the kidney and using a tin of chuck steak obtained from Marks and Spencer. This reduces cooking time to about 1 hour because the tinned steak is already cooked. I also give the pastry a bit of 'interest' by adding some cut-up pieces of fried bacon. For a richer gravy use half water and half Guinness."

OUR SCOTTISH KNITWEAR CONTAINS ONLY THE PUREST OF INGREDIENTS

SCOTTISH CASHMERE • FINE KNITWEAR

BY APPOINTMENT TO
HER MAJESTY THE QUEEN
MANUFACTURERS OF
KNITTED GARMENTS
PRINGLE OF SCOTLAND LTD

BY APPOINTMENT TO
HER MAJESTY QUEEN ELIZABETH
THE QUEEN MOTHER
MANUFACTURERS OF KNITTED GARMENTS
PRINGLE OF SCOTLAND LTD

Pringle OF SCOTLAND

BRAEMAR
SCOTTISH·KNITWEAR

Ballantyne

barrie

McGeorge

Glenmac
KNITWEAR HAWICK SCOTLAND

Gladstone

DAWSON INTERNATIONAL PLC
9 CHARLOTTE SQUARE EDINBURGH EH2 4DR

MABEL COTTON'S STEAK AND KIDNEY PUDDING

Bill Cotton

INGREDIENTS

pastry:
12 oz plain flour.
6 oz fresh suet.
salt and pepper.
water to mix.
filling:
1½ lb chuck steak (cubes 1½" square).
½ lb ox kidney chopped.
1 large onion.
2 Oxo cubes.
warm water.
seasoned flour.

Mix the flour and finely chopped fresh suet, salt and pepper. Flour pastry board. Roll our ⅔ pastry and line well-buttered pudding basin.

Roll meat in seasoned flour, put in layers, with onion and crumbled oxo cube, into basin lined with pastry until almost full. Fill with warm water. Roll out remaining ⅓ pastry and press onto top. Cover with buttered greaseproof paper with pleat in the middle to allow for expansion, cover with cloth and tie on lightly with string. Bring corners of cloth together over the top of the basin and tie a knot.

Put the remaining meat and onion and oxo cube into a casserole and cover with warm water. Simmer slowly to add extra juice to completed pudding.

Put boiling water into saucepan and gently lower pudding basin into it. Make sure it is covered with water. Boil for 4 hours, occasionally topping up with boiling water.

Lift out saucepan, remove cloth and greaseproof paper and serve.

STUFFED CABBAGE

Claire Rayner

———— Serves 6 ————

INGREDIENTS

6 large cabbage leaves.
1 lb (450 g) minced beef.
2 onions grated.
3 oz (80 g) uncooked rice.
salt and pepper.
garlic and herbs.
1 egg.
chicken or beef stock.

Cabbage leaves are carefully removed from the parent plant and put in very hot water for a while to soften them. The stuffing I use is minced beef mixed together with grated onion, seasoned with salt and pepper, garlic and the herb of your choice. I used marjoram. I also added a handful of uncooked rice and bound the lot together with a beaten egg.

Each leaf is then given a dollop of meat and rice and packed into a neat little parcel, with the corners folded in firmly. Arrange the parcels tidily in an oven dish so that they really are packed tight, and then pour over the top some very concentrated chicken or beef stock. Some people add tomato puree, brown sugar and a tablespoonful of vinegar at this stage, to make the dish sweet and sour. I prefer it this plainer way. Bake the parcels, covered, in a warm to moderate oven Reg 3-4, 325-350°F/170-180°C for about 1 hour or even two, to make sure the rice is cooked through. They're marvellously filling, taste as good as they look, and if you've any left over, they can be frozen very successfully.

Alternative stuffings:
1. Breadcrumbs, minced ham and sage.
2. Minced lamb, pearl barley, *bouquet garni.*
3. Minced lamb, lentils and split peas, bayleaf.
4. Minced liver, oatmeal, *herbes de Provence.*

VINDALOO

This dish, as far as can be discovered, was first concocted by Portugese settlers in India, now brought to perfection by their descendents, the Goanese.

———— Serves 6 ————

INGREDIENTS

2 lbs of pork, beef or a duck.
6 oz ghee, lard, dripping or mustard oil (mustard oil preferably).
1 tablespoon mashed garlic cloves.
1 tablespoon ground ginger.
1 teaspoon ground chilli.
1 teaspoon ground coriander.
½ tspn ground cumin.
3 bayleaves.
12 peppercorns.
6 cloves (ground).
5 cardamon (ground).
6 small sticks cinnamon (ground)
– 2" long each stick.
4 oz malt vinegar.
½ teaspoon salt.

Cut beef or pork into large cubes, or duck into pieces. Mix vinegar and all ground condiments, plus ½ teaspoon salt thoroughly.

Steep the meat or duck in this concoction for 18 – 24 hours (24 hours preferably).

Heat fat in thick pan. Toss in the meat, condiments and vinegar. Add peppercorn plus bayleaves.

Simmer gently over slow heat for 2 hours, until meat is tender, then turn out and serve up hot with rice and accompaniments.

Acker Bilk

"When we were staying in Singapore to do a concert a bloke in the hotel, the Entertainments Manager, Mr Mercier, took us out for an authentic Chinese meal in China Town. There were about 12 or 13 courses, and one of these courses particularly appealed to me. I thought it was really lovely, then it turned out to be snake! I felt sick for the rest of the night."

Poultry

BILL OWEN'S FAVOURITE CHICKEN

INGREDIENTS

4 chicken breast fillets.
1 large onion.
2 rashers lean bacon.
1 glass dry white wine.
1 egg yolk.
2 cloves garlic.
bouquet garni.
1 oz butter.
$1/4$ pint double cream.

Grill chicken gently till cooked but not brown.

Meanwhile fry onion (chopped finely) and bacon (also chopped finely) in butter until cooked but not brown. Add crushed garlic and bouquet garni and wine. Reduce wine to about half and add cooked chicken. Simmer gently for a few minutes. Beat yolk into cream and then add to chicken mixture, do not boil as it will curdle. Stir gently until sauce is thickened, remove bouquet garni, season with salt and pepper, but only if required (the bacon should give it enough salt, so taste first).

Serve with a green vegetable and mashed potatoes.

Bill Owen

CHICKEN AND LEEK PIE

——— Serve hot ———

INGREDIENTS

1 boiling chicken.
1 onion.
1 bayleaf and seasoning.
4 good size leeks.
$^{1}/_{4}$ lb (110 g) cooked tongue.
$^{1}/_{4}$ pint (150 ml) double cream.
8 oz (225 g) shortcrust pastry.

Boil chicken with onion, bayleaf and seasoning until tender and leave to cool.

Grease an ovenproof dish with butter. Cut cooked chicken into 1" (2.5 cm) long pieces, cut leeks into rounds, then place one layer of chicken pieces in prepared dish, season, then one layer of leeks. Continue placing layers of chicken and of leeks alternately until ingredients are used. Cover with a layer of cooked tongue, use stock from boiled chicken to fill, leaving enough space for expansion. Cover the pie dish with shortcrust pastry.

Bake in a hot oven 375° Gas Mark 5, for 30 minutes. Remove from oven, make a hole in the pastry crust and pour in the warmed double cream, replace in oven for 15 minutes. Serve hot.

Michael Crawford OBE

Best Wish MLDCrawford

CHICKEN BREASTS IN GARLIC CREAM SAUCE

Thelma Barlow

INGREDIENTS

¹/₂ oz butter.
1 tablespoon vegetable oil.
¹/₂ small onion peeled and very finely chopped.
4 garlic cloves, peeled and crushed.
¹/₂ pint double cream.
salt and freshly ground black pepper.
6 skinned chicken breast halves.

Heat oil and butter in a large saucepan. Cook onion until transparent. Add garlic and cream, season with salt and pepper. Bring to boil, stirring, turn heat to very low.

Place chicken breasts in pan (1 layer if possible), cover and cook for 10 minutes on low heat, turning once. Check chicken is cooked through, but do not overcook. Transfer to hot plates and coat with garlic cream sauce.

Serve with steamed brocoli over which is poured melted butter and flacked or slivered almonds.

CHICKEN HAWAIIN SALAD

INGREDIENTS

4 oz almonds.
1 cooked roasting chicken
(about 2-2$\frac{1}{2}$ lb).
1 fresh pineapple.
1 green pepper.
1 head of chicory.
$\frac{1}{4}$-$\frac{1}{2}$ pint mayonnaise.
lettuce.
for garnish:
tomatoes, cucumber, celery or extra
chicory.

Blanch almonds and brown under the grill or in oven. Dice the cooked chicken. Cut the top off the pineapple (keep the leaves in good green condition). Cut the pineapple into rings. Cut away the skin and core the slices. Do this over a basin to catch the juice. Dice the pineapple. Blend most of the almonds, the chicken, pineapple, diced green pepper (discard core and seeds) and chopped chicory.

Blend the required amount of mayonnaise with some pineapple juice. Toss the chicken mixture in this pile on a bed of lettuce, sprinkle with remaining almonds, garnish with quartered tomatoes, sliced cucumber, diced celery and chicory leaves. Top the salad with the pineapple leaves.

Can be varied by replacing pineapple with other fruit (ie oranges, bananas, fresh peaches or nectarines.

Marilyn and Ian Bannen

CHICKEN TIKKA

Serves 4

INGREDIENTS

4 chicken breasts (8 pieces).
4 tablespoons vinegar.
2 fresh lemons.
½ tablespoon salt.
1 fresh ginger.
2 whole garlics.
15 sprays of fresh coriander.
8 green chillis.
1 green pepper.
6 oz mustard oil.
1 pint natural yoghurt.
1 tablespoon unsweetened mint.
¼ tablespoon chilli powder.
1 teaspoon carraway seeds.
2 tablespoons cumin seeds.
¼ teaspoon yellow colouring.

Remove skin and dice chicken breasts. Wash thoroughly and dry. Add fresh lemon, vinegar, salt and leave for 20 minutes.

Take fresh ginger, garlic, coriander, green chillis, green pepper, lemon and mustard oil. Grind them and paste chicken pieces. When this is ready, leave for one hour.

Mix yoghurt with the mint, yellow colouring, chilli powder, carraway seeds and cumin seeds. Mix marinated chicken slices into yoghurt and leave for 1 hour.

NB: It is not important that this is cooked in a Tandoori oven. It can successfully be cooked on a grill with tinfoil.

Serve with salad and mint yoghurt.

Mint Yoghurt (for 4 people)
Mix 1½ pint yoghurt, 1 tablespoon mint, 1 tablespoon sugar. Blend contents of 1 oz tin of lycee and 1 oz tin of mango. Add pinch of salt and 1 pinch of red chilli.

Asha Tandoori Restaurant Edinburgh

Safraz Rathore is the proprietor of Asha Tandoori Restaurant, 8 West Maitland Street, Edinburgh, was born in the Lahore (Pakistan). He got his Master Degree from Punjab University and came to this country in 1975. He opened his restaurant seven years ago and in 1987 helped to organise the catering at the immensely successful Oriental Ball, held at the Royal Museum of Scotland in aid of charity.

CHICKEN TROPICANA

Gillian Taylforth

———— Serves 2-4 ————

INGREDIENTS

marinade:
3 tablespoons of malt vinegar.
$^{1}/_{2}$ teaspoon soya sauce.
2 teaspoons honey.
pinch ground ginger.
juice of 1 x 8 oz can pineapple rings.
$2^{1}/_{2}$ fl oz tomato juice.

4 medium chicken joints (skinned).
$^{1}/_{2}$ oz butter.
1 large carrot cut into strips.
1 x 8 oz can pineapple rings (juice
drained for above).
2 level teaspoons cornflour.
salt and pepper to taste.

Mix together the ingredients for the marinade, place the chicken joints in a dish. Pour over the marinade and chill for at least 4 hours (covered). Turn the joints occasionally.

Heat the butter in a frying pan. Remove the chicken joints from the marinade and fry in the butter for about 15 minutes or until almost cooked. Add the carrot strips and pineapple, cut into pieces and fry for a further 2 minutes.

Blend the marinade into the cornflour, pour over the chicken. Bring to the boil then simmer for 5 minutes.

Serve with rice and vegetables.

CHICKEN WOODCOTE

Rt Hon Edward Heath MBE, MP

Serves 4

INGREDIENTS

8 chicken thighs.
3 tablespoons olive oil.
1/2 lb button mushrooms.
1 glass white wine.
1 small tin tomatoes (chopped).
1 tablespoon chopped parsley.
1 garlic clove crushed.
1/2 cup chicken stock.
salt and pepper.

Saute the chicken in the olive oil. Add the mushrooms and cook slowly together, with the lid on, turning occasionally. When cooked, remove chicken and mushrooms to a fireproof dish to keep warm. Add the remaining ingredients to the pan, stir well allowing to cook rapidly and reduce liquid a little. Strain the sauce over the chicken and sprinkle with chopped parsley.

Serve with new potatoes and broccoli.

FAMILY TURKEY PIE

Brian Clough

—————— Serves 4 ——————

INGREDIENTS

rough puff or shortcrust pastry.
2 oz streaky bacon.
1 medium sized onion chopped.
1 oz margarine.
1 oz plain flour.
1/4 pint turkey stock or chicken stock
cube in 1/4 pint boiling water.
1/4 pint milk.
8 oz cooked turkey chopped.
1 tablespoon lemon juice.
1 pinch nutmeg.
salt and pepper.

De-rind bacon and fry the rinds to extract fat. Remove rinds from pan and add bacon, cut into small pieces, chopped onion and fry until lightly browned. Keep hot. Melt margarine in pan, stir in flour. Gradually add the stock and milk and bring to the boil, stirring all the time. Add turkey, bacon, onion, lemon juice, nutmeg, salt and pepper. Stir well. Cover and allow to cool. Make up the pie in the usual way. Brush top with beaten egg. Bake at Reg 6/7, 400°F/200°C for about 30 minutes, just above the centre of the oven.

"I personally enjoy cooking very much, and have enclosed a recipe which I both enjoy to make and eat. A good, filling pie, and one which I shall find very useful after Christmas!"

HAWAIIAN CHICKEN

Serves 4

INGREDIENTS

2 medium fryers – cut up.
$1/4$ cup butter.
2 tablespoons flour.
1 cup orange juice.
1 small can condensed chicken broth.
1 teaspoon salt, dash cayenne, cinnamon
and garlic salt.
1 20 oz can pineapple chunks.
$1/2$ cup raisins.
2 oz slivered blanched almonds.

Brown chicken pieces in melted butter in large Dutch oven or heavy skillet. Remove chicken as it browns. Pour off all but 4 tablespoons fat. Stir in flour and cook and stir for 5 minutes. Gradually stir in orange juice and broth. Return chicken to Dutch oven – add salt, cayenne, cinnamon, pineapple, liquid and raisins. Cover and simmer over low heat for 50- 60 minutes, or until chicken is tender.

Sprinkle with almonds. Garnish with parsley and orange slices.

Henry Winkler

"Here is a recipe that has been in my family's cookbook for a long time. It has given my mouth a party for many a year. I hope you enjoy it too!"

87

PASTA ALLA AMATRICIANA

— Serves 4 —

INGREDIENTS

12 rashers bacon, unsmoked sliced crossways.
2 15 oz tins peeled tomatoes.
garlic.
2 medium sized onions.
thyme.
1 chicken stock cube.
parmigiano cheese for grating.

Fry bacon in two tablespoons of olive oil then remove and keep warm. Peel the clove of garlic, lay the flat of a knife blade on top and give it a thump with your fist. After you've bandaged your hand, add the split clove to the oil and saute. After a few moments discard it. Garlic is a natural flavour enhancer; neither the dish nor you should reek of it! Now add the finely chopped onions to the oil and sprinkle with a pinch of thyme. Saute. Before onion burns, add the tomatoes. Do not pour them straight from the tin, but first crush them. The gadget for mashing potatoes is excellent for this.

Boil one cupful of water and dissolve a chicken stock cube. Add this to the pan. Season with black pepper – but no salt, the stock cube supplies that. Simmer gently without a lid for 10-15 minutes, stirring occasionally. The final sauce should be niether watery nor pasty.

When ready, grate in some parmigiano cheese (parmesan) and stir. Never, never buy pre-grated parmigiano, it smells like vomit! A piece of parmigiano keeps for a long time, simply wrapped in brown paper and kept in a larder – or larder part of your fridge.

The Pasta:
You can of course use any of the pasta shapes. The two I prefer are plain spaghetti or penne which are little tubes about 1$^1/_2$" long. You must use a lot of

Tom Conti

water to boil pasta – I would never cook pasta for 4 in less than 12 pints of water with a tablespoon of salt. For the penne 8 pints would probably be enough. I'm talking about Italian portions here, about 6 oz per person (dry weight).

Don't overcook the pasta. It should be "al dente" that is, slightly firm at the centre. Start tasting pieces after 5 minutes boiling. Every brand has a different cooking time and never go by what it says on the packet. When you drain the pasta into the colander, be careful that it doesn't slide backwards out of it into the sink!

Just before serving, return the bacon to the sauce and mix.

When served, grate parmigiano and put black pepper on top.

There is no tidy way to eat spaghetti. You must forget that you are British. Wind some onto the fork and put it in your mouth. Bite off the hanging bits and let them fall back onto the plate, you'll get them next time. Don't let pathetically silly things like "table manners" spoil your enjoyment of one of the world's truly great dishes. Drink red wine with this – unless you're driving. Soda with a dash of lime cordial seems to go very well.

PEACOCK PIE

Chris Clyne

My clothes are always being described as rich and exotic, therefore I always like to make a surprise with a dish as fabled as peacock pie.

Obtaining a peacock is rarely a problem. One of the nice things about some of my best clients is that they tend to have several of the birds pecking around outside their orangeries and they always let me have one for the oven for special occasions.

Sending the bird out of this life is never a problem since I have so many friends who cannot bear the noise they make. So, having put it to sleep for ever, all you have to do is to pluck and draw the bird as with any other. Make sure to save the long tail feathers which will be required later.

Lightly roast the peacock in a hot oven with lots of fat for one hour. Allow to cool and then pull it to shreds. Save the bones for peacock soup and place all the flesh in a large pie dish. Fill the dish up so that the flesh is completely covered with alcohol of your choice. I usually use brandy, but I know those who swear by calvados, and marinate for two days.

Cover with short crust pastry, leaving enough pastry to cut small peacocks out for decoration on the top of the pie and cook in a medium oven for 45 minutes. When ready, use the tail feathers to make a crown on top. Trim the dish below with a frilled skirt of peacock blue net. Serve with chestnut stuffing on the side.

The sight of the final product being carried into the dining room can be guaranteed to produce cries of delight mingled with horror from your guests. I have never quite decided which they are.

If there are not enough tail feathers there will always be a fight as to who gets to take one home with them, so do make sure to provide one for each of the guests.

We never argue about the skirt.

ROAST PHEASANT

INGREDIENTS

Choose nice tender young birds – check
that the spurs are short (long spurs mean
an older bird).

Remove the giblets and mix the liver with
3 or 3 petits suisses fresh cheeses,
together with chopped sage (dried or
fresh, preferably), salt and pepper.
Put this mixture in the cavity of the
bird(s). Salt and pepper the pheasant and
place streaky bacon along the breast and
legs. Remove after $^1/_2$ hour to brown top.
Roast in a hot oven for about $^3/_4$-1 hour,
depending on the size, until the juices run
clear.

Remove the birds and make the gravy by
removing any fat left behind, stirring
some vegetable stock into the pan.
A little port could be added if wanted,
and although the gravy should not be
thick, a little flour can be mixed into the
juices before adding the main liquid.

Serve with braised red cabbage, bread
sauce, game chips, roast potatoes and
sprouts.

Jimmy Hill

STIR-FRIED CHICKEN IN BLACK BEAN SAUCE

Gemma Craven

— Serves 2 —

INGREDIENTS

8 oz boneless chicken breast.
2 sticks celery.
2 carrots.
1/2 small green pepper.
1/2 small red pepper.
1 tablespoon oil.
1 oz cashew nuts.
5 fl oz jar Cantonese black bean sauce.

Remove any skin from the chicken. Cut meat into thin strips. Slice celery diagonally. Peel carrots and cut into matchsticks. Core and de-seed peppers. Cut into long strips. Heat oil in a wok or large frying pan until hazing. Add chicken and stir fry for 2 minutes. Add celery and carrots. Stir fry for a further minute. Add peppers and cashews, then the black bean sauce. Cook, stirring for 2 minutes. Serve immediately with boiled rice.

TIP: Get the pan really hot first, then 'dig and toss' furiously. Minimal cooking keeps the food crisp and fresh.

TURKEY AU GRATIN WITH ALMONDS

Tom O'Connor

To transform cold turkey into a delicious dish. (Can be made in advance and cooked when you need it or kept hot in a low oven for up to 3 hours before serving).

——————— Serves 6-8 ———————

INGREDIENTS

2 lb cooked turkey.
1 oz butter.
4 oz blanched flaked almonds.

sauce:
2 oz butter.
2 oz flour.
1¼ pints milk.
4 tablespoons sherry.
2 large cloves garlic.
6 oz cheddar cheese.
salt and ground black pepper.
grated parmesan cheese to sprinkle.
watercress or parsley to decorate.

Set oven at 325°F/160°C (Gas Mark 3). Cut the turkey into bite-sized pieces and arrange into a large, shallow, ovenproof dish. Melt butter in a frying pan, add almonds and cook over a high heat for 2-3 minutes, tossing almonds continuously until they are golden. Spoon over the turkey pieces.

To make sauce:
Melt the butter in a medium pan, add flour and cook for 1 minute. Remove from heat and gradually add milk, stirring well between each addition. Return to heat and bring to the boil, stirring continuously. Cook for 1 minute. Add sherry. Peel and crush garlic cloves and coarsely grate cheddar. Stir into the sauce with salt and pepper. Pour sauce over turkey, sprinkle with parmesan cheese. Cook in the centre of the oven for 30-45 minutes until golden brown and bubbly.

Garnish with watercress or parsley and serve immediately with a green salad.

WHICKER'S CHINESE CHICKEN

Serves 4

INGREDIENTS

2 cups chicken breast, cut into $\frac{1}{2}''$ slices.
marinade for chicken:
1 tablespoon light soya sauce.
1 tablespoon sherry.
1 tablespoon cornflour.
$\frac{1}{2}$ teaspoon each sugar and salt.
8 oz peas, fresh or frozen.
6 oz celery diced.
6 oz onions diced.
4 to 8 oz whole almonds.
1 $2\frac{1}{2}$ oz can whole button mushrooms
(reserve liquid).
6 oz red pepper diced.
sauce mixture:
$\frac{1}{2}$ cup reserved mushroom liquid.
2 teaspoons cornflour.
1 teaspoon light soya sauce.
1 clove garlic crushed.
1 chunk ginger, the size of a 1p, crushed.
4 tablespoons oil.

Mix sliced chicken with marinade and let stand for 15 minutes. Prepare sauce mixture.

Heat wok, pour in 1 tablespoon oil and heat. Stir-fry celery and onions for 1-2 minutes. Season lightly with salt and sugar. Set aside. Add 1 tablespoon oil and stir-fry peas with red peppers for 1-2 minutes; also season lightly with salt and sugar. Set aside. Add 2 tablespoons oil and brown crushed garlic and ginger for 1 minute. Discard and stir-fry chicken until done. Stir the prepared sauce mixture and pour over chicken, stirring until sauce thickens. Add vegetables, then add almonds. Mix well and serve.

Alan Whicker

good luck!

Vegetarian

CARROTT CURRY

Jasper Carrot

—— Serves 4 ——

INGREDIENTS

4 carrots sliced.
3 large potatoes diced.
2 medium sized onions sliced.
1 small swede diced.
4 tablespoons peanut oil
or melted butter.
1½ teaspoons salt.
1½ teaspoons turmeric.
1 tablespoon cumin seeds.
½ teaspoon cinnamon.
1 teaspoon coriander (ground).
¾ pint (425 ml) water.
¼ pint (150 ml) plain yoghurt.
5 oz (150 g) frozen peas (defrosted).

Heat the oil (or butter) in a large saucepan; when it is warm, add all the spices. Simmer for about 3 minutes then add all the vegetables, stir immediately to coat them with the spices. Keep stirring for about 5 minutes on a low heat. Put the water in, and simmer all the ingredients for about ½ hour, stirring occasionally. If the vegetables are tender, stir in the yoghurt and the peas. Cook for about another 10 minutes on a lowish heat.

Serve with saffron rice.

CHEESE AND WALNUT ROAST

—— Serves 4 ——

INGREDIENTS

8 oz walnuts.
6 oz fresh brown breadcrumbs.
3 oz cheddar cheese, finely grated.
1 medium onion, finely grated.
2 level teaspoons salt.
2 level teaspoons finely chopped parsley.
mixed herbs to taste.
5 tablespoons hot milk.
1 level teaspoon prepared mustard.
1 level tablespoon tomato paste.
pepper to taste.
$^1/_2$ oz polyunsaturated margarine.

Preheat oven to moderate (350°F/180°C or Gas Mark 4). Line baking tray with foil and grease lightly.

Grind nuts and mix thoroughly with all other ingredients except margarine. Shape into loaf approx 3" high and stand it on prepared tray. Dot top with flakes of margarine and bake in centre of oven for 45 minutes.

Serve sliced

Cleo Laine

CRESPELLE RIPIENE

Sue Lawley

— Serves 4 —

INGREDIENTS

pancake batter:
scant 4 oz/125 g plain flour.
¼ teaspoon salt.
2 small eggs.
1 tablespoon oil.
¼ pint/150 ml milk.
6 tablespoons water.
filling:
8 oz/250 g frozen chopped spinach,
cooked and squeezed dry.
8 oz/250 g ricotta or curd cheese.
1 oz/25 g grated parmesan cheese.
1 egg beaten.
grated nutmeg, salt and pepper.
topping:
1 oz/25 g butter.
3 tablespoons grated parmesan cheese.
5 tablespoons chicken stock.

Sift the flour and salt into a bowl. Make a well in the centre and add the eggs, oil and milk. Beat until smooth then stir in the water. Cover and chill for 1 to 2 hours.

Lightly oil a 7" (18 cm) frying pan and place over heat. When hot, pour in just enough batter to cover the base. When the pancake is set and the underside lightly browned, turn and briefly cook the other side. Repeat with the remaining batter, making 8 pancakes.

Mix the filling ingredients together, seasoning liberally with nutmeg, salt and pepper. Divide between the pancakes, roll up loosely and arrange in a buttered ovenproof dish. Dot with the butter, sprinkle with the parmesan cheese and pour in the stock.

Bake in a preheated moderately hot oven (400°F/200°C), Gas Mark 6, for about 20 minutes until golden. Serve immediately.

DAUPHINOISE A LA HAY

Scrub 2 or 3 large potatoes. Cut them in 1/4" slices. Place in an inch of water, salted. Chop 1 large onion, put in with potatoes and boil for 8-10 minutes. Place in oven proof dish along with any remaining water then pour over double cream to cover, then a drop more! Place in hot oven, Gas Mark 4 to 5, and bake until browned (about 3/4 hour).

Smashing with salad.

ENTHUSIASTIC STEW

INGREDIENTS

Put everything you've got into it! Cut up any vegetables you can get given.

Melt 2 oz margarine in large saucepan. Throw in vegetables, onions first and saute over moderate heat for 5 minutes. Add stock, soya sauce, garlic to taste. Increase heat and bring to boil. Turn down heat and simmer for at least 1 hour.

Bill Treacher

Bill Maynard

98

LEEK AND NOODLE CASSEROLE

—— Serves 4 ——

Boil 350 g of wholemeal noodles in salted water (with a little oil) until soft, then drain.

Cut four or five leeks into ½" pieces, wash, and then saute in a large pan with some oil and water. Add a small amount of granulated vegetable stock and curry powder to give a very mild taste. Cook until soft but not coloured.

Place in a casserole dish in alternate layers of leeks and noodles. As a fifth layer, cover with grated cheese and pour over this some single cream. Bake in a hot oven until crisp and golden – approximately 20 minutes.

HRH
The Prince of Wales

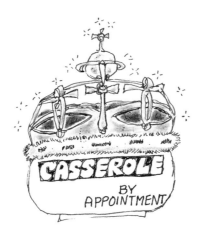

SOYABURGERS IN TOMATO SAUCE

—— Serves 4 ——

INGREDIENTS

1 lb (455 g) soya beans, cooked, drained
and mashed.
1/2 lb (225 g) brown rice.
1 onion minced.
1 small carrot grated.
4 oz (115 g) wholemeal breadcrumbs.
2 tablespoons soya sauce.
1 egg or 1/4 pint (140 ml) soya milk.
2 oz (55 g) wholemeal flour.
seasoning to taste (eg herbs, garlic or
curry powder, cumin).
vegetable oil for frying.

Combine all the ingredients together and
knead the mixture for a couple of
minutes to bind it.

Shape the mixture into patties and deep
or shallow fry them in the oil, turning
them once.

Serve with tomato sauce and stir-fry
vegetables.

TOMATO SAUCE

INGREDIENTS:

4 fresh tomatoes.
1/2 tin peeled tomatoes.
1 stock cube.
1 tablespoon olive oil.
1 tablespoon butter.
1 carrot finely chopped.
1 stick celery.
1 onion finely chopped.
1 teaspoon honey.
1 tablespoon tomato purée.

Place all ingredients in a pan and simmer
until soft.

Jackie Stewart

Liquidise.
Add salt, pepper and freshly chopped
basil to taste.

WATERSIDE INN

The management and staff of the Waterside Inns Ltd wish the
Leukaemia & Cancer Children's Fund every success in their fund raising.
At the same time we invite you to try two mouth watering recipes from the
award winning team in our kitchens.

TOURNEDOS DE VEAU 'ROLENE'
(Fillet of veal in a piquant rasberry brandy sauce)

INGREDIENTS

1½ lb fillet of veal
3 fl oz raspberry brandy
½ pint demi glace
½ fl oz vinegar
3 oz butter
12 oz carrots
3 oz cream cheese
1 oz chives
1 lb potatoes
½ bunch watercress
½ oz caster sugar
4 slices white bread

Trim veal fillets and cut into small steaks. Season.

Saute in butter and keep warm.

Add raspberry brandy to pan. Add demi glace and vinegar. Reduce to correct consistency and adjust seasoning.

Make croutons with bread and fry in a little butter. Serve Tournedos on croutons and coat with sauce.

Garnish with watercress.

Serve with turned carrots glace and potato nests with cream cheese and chives.

Demi glace is a basic, thickened brown sauce, made with vegetables and meat stock.

CHOCOLATE DE FRAISE 'SUNDART'
(A light strawberry mousse on a chocolate shell decorated with piped chocolate)

INGREDIENTS

12 oz strawberries
¼ pint double cream
½ oz (4 sheets) gelatine
3 oz chocolate
drops glycerine
2 eggs
½ oz icing sugar
1 fl oz kirsch
5 fl oz milk
1 oz caster sugar

Puree strawberries through a fine sieve.

Soak leaf gelatine.

Boil milk and dissolve gelatine.

Whisk egg yolks and caster sugar and add to milk. Put to set over ice. When just setting, fold in whisked egg whites, whipped cream and strawberry puree. Set in dariole moulds.

Melt chocolate and add a little glycerine. Pipe into shell shapers and curve. Also pipe decorations for top.

Mix a little strawberry puree, kirsch and icing sugar for sauce on plates. Put a little sauce on to plate, then make a spider's web with a thin line of cream (feathered), pull through with a cocktail stick. Turn out mousse on to chocolate shells.

Decorate top with a fresh strawberry and piped chocolate.

ARDOE·HOUSE
HOTEL

To make your reservations contact us at:

Waterside Inn, Fraserburgh Road, Peterhead, AB4 7BN · Tel: 0779 71121 · Telex: 739413
Ardoe House Hotel, South Deeside Road, Blairs, Aberdeen, AB1 5YP · Tel: 0224 867355 · Fax: 0224 861283

"I STARTED WITH STORK
AND ENDED UP WITH JACK NICHOLSON."

"My husband is very partial to my steak and stout pie. He says there's something about my pastry that makes it light and crisp every time. Well, that's because I always get a little help from Stork.

Stork rubs in so well. And when I've made the pastry, I pop it in the fridge for 15 minutes. It's a little trick that helps reduce the shrinkage when I come to roll the pastry out.

After the pie last week, my husband asked if I wanted to go and see the latest Jack Nicholson film.

Well, I don't have to be asked twice to see my favourite film star!

I noticed there's another great film coming to the cinema next week. Looks like another job for Stork!"

Mrs D. Hodges

If you've got a Stork® story with a difference, please write to: Stork Cookery Service, Van den Berghs, Sussex House, Burgess Hill, West Sussex, RH15 9AW.

The difference is worth talking about.

STUFFED PEPPERS

Mike Yarwood

——— Serves 4 ———

INGREDIENTS

4 firm peppers (green).
2 oz butter.
2 rashers streaky bacon chopped.
1 onion finely chopped.
2 tomatoes skinned and chopped.
2 oz long grain rice cooked.
$^{1}/_{4}$ teaspoon mixed herbs.
salt and pepper.
4 oz cheddar cheese.

Pre-heat oven to 350°F (Gas Mark 4).

Cut a slice off the top of each pepper, then remove centre core and seeds. Stand peppers upright in an ovenproof dish.

Melt butter in a saucepan. Add bacon and onions then fry gently until soft. Add tomatoes, rice, mixed herbs, salt and pepper. Pile mixture into pepper shells. Top each one with grated cheese.

Bake for 30-40 minutes until peppers are tender.

Serve hot.

"The date was 15th November 1972. I remember it quite clearly as my wife Sandra, was nine months pregnant with our second daughter Claire. We were having a Chinese meal in a restaurant with my parents and my sister and her husband. Unknown to me at the time, Sandra was having 'twinges,' which she suspected might be the baby. Knowing that if she had said anything, we would have dashed her off to the hospital, and she would have missed her dinner, she finished her meal before telling me.
Clare was born at 7.20 the following morning, and we all laughed as we were sure she had a decidedly Chinese look about her!"

VEGETABLES IN WHITE SAUCE

—— Serves 6 ——

INGREDIENTS

2 medium sized potatoes.
2 medium sized parsnips.
$\frac{1}{2}$ cauliflower.
a few florets of broccoli.
1 large courgette.
1 large onion.
2 carrots.
1 clove garlic.
1 small spoon of wholemeal flour.
1 vegetable stock cube.
$\frac{1}{2}$ pint water.
seasoning to taste.
1 tablespoon of vegetable oil for frying.
1 small green chilli with the seeds
removed (optional).

Any other seasonal vegetables may be used instead or as well as the vegetables above.

Peel and slice the potatoes, onion, carrots and clove of garlic. Steam the parsnips, cauliflower and carrots together. When they are half cooked, add the potatoes and broccoli for 10 minutes. Add the courgette. Cook until just soft. Keep the potatoes separate. Chop the onion and garlic and saute in the oil until soft. Remove from heat and add the wholemeal flour. Stir until smooth, add the stock gradually and keep stirring to keep it smooth.

As I like my food very spicy, I add the green chilli with the seeds removed and chopped very finely.

Mix the vegetables with the sauce. Put the sliced potatoes on the top of the vegetables, brush them with a little oil and put the dish in the oven on medium heat until they are brown.

Serve steaming hot as an accompaniment or on it's own.

Lulu

VEGETABLE TARTS

Barbara Dickson

—— Serves 4 ——

INGREDIENTS

½ lb shortcrust pastry.
2 oz grated cheddar cheese.
½ pint of white sauce.
Salt and pepper.
1 egg yolk.
1 tablespoon lemon juice.
8 flowerets cooked cauliflower.
1 cup cooked diced carrot.
1 cup cooked green peas.
1 cooked whole onion.

Roll out the pastry and sprinkle it with cheese, fold and roll it out again. Grease the insides of the tartlet tins. Cut the pastry into sizes to cover the insides of the tins and cook in a hot oven (Mark 7) for 15-20 mins. Add beaten egg yolk and salt and pepper to the white sauce and stir over a low heat for a few minutes and then add the lemon juice. Mix the cooked vegetables with the white sauce. Remove the tartlet cases from the tins and fill with vegetable mixture. Serve them piping hot. They can be placed under grill for quick browning.

A buttery taste which puts you in Clover.

Like butter, Clover is made with fresh cream. We simply add some vegetable oil. So the only difference you'll notice is the way it spreads. Not the way it tastes.

Clover is the perfect choice for your favourite recipes too. It creams quickly and easily for delicious cakes and tasty sauces.

Clover can be heated to a higher temperature than butter, so it's ideal for sautéing and frying.

And for scrumptious puddings and desserts there's a slightly salted version.

For low-calorie cooking try delicious Clover Light. Spread it or cook with it. Any way you'll be in Clover.

Pasta

CARBONARA

Terry Butcher

—— Serves 4 ——

INGREDIENTS

8 oz tagliatelle.
1 pint double cream.
1 clove garlic.
4 oz parma ham.
salt.
pepper.
1 oz butter.
1 oz chopped fresh herbs.

Cook tagliatelle in salted water till aldente (undercooked). Refresh in cold water.

Crush garlic clove. Sweat in $\frac{1}{2}$ oz butter. Add double cream. Bring to boil. Reduce by half till correct consistency. Slice parma ham in strips and blanch in boiling water. Add parma ham to garlic cream. Add pasta to garlic cream. Heat through. Adjust seasoning. Sprinkle with chopped herbs and serve.

LO MANAZATTI

Michael Fish

--- Serves 10 ---

INGREDIENTS

2 lbs lean pork cut in small pieces.
8 onions sliced.
1 large jar tomato puree.
2 cups of water.
$^3/_4$ lb mushrooms sliced.
1 tin creamed mushrooms
or condensed mushroom soup.
2 green peppers sliced.
1 lb strong cheddar cheese cubed.
salt, pepper cayenne.
1 oz margarine.
1 packet shell noodles.

Melt the margarine, brown the onions and pork and put into large mixing bowl. Add all the other ingredients except the noodles.

Boil the noodles for 15 minutes, strain well and add to mixture. Put into a large casserole, grate some cheese on top. Put into a pre-heated oven (350°F 180°C) for one hour.

This is delicious with a tossed green salad and garlic bread.

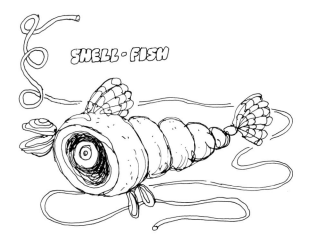

SHELL·FISH

Pears Soap
Pure and Gentle

Using only natural ingredients, Pears Soap has been made in the same way
for nearly 200 years, providing pure and gentle care for all the family.

MY PASTA
(PASTA CASA NOSTA)

———— Serves 5-6 ————

INGREDIENTS

olive oil.
2 or 3 cloves garlic.
1 onion (optional).
2 or 3 bayleaves.
oregano to taste.
salt and freshly ground pepper.
1 lb tomatoes (or 2 tins of tomatoes or a mixture of fresh and tinned tomatoes).
black olives to taste.
1 green pepper.
$1/2$ red pepper (if you have them).
$1/2$ lb mushrooms (if liked).
dash of concentrated tomato paste.
– and anything else you'd like it to taste of . . . .
large packet of fresh pasta – my favourite is green tagliatelli.

Into a pan of boiling water to which you've added a teaspoon of olive oil, drop the pasta. About 5 minutes does it.

Meanwhile add chopped tomatoes, the herbs, and all, or some, of the other ingredients. If you have half a glass of wine handy, add that too.

Serve separately with plenty of freshly grated cheese.

Susannah York

SAUCY PASTA SPIRALS

Maria Whittaker

———— Serves 4 ————

INGREDIENTS

1 lb (500 g) lean Scotch minced beef.
4 rashers streaky bacon chopped.
1 tablespoon (15 ml) oil (if needed).
1 large onion finely chopped.
1 garlic clove crushed.
1 small green or red pepper finely chopped.
1 large carrot finely sliced.
$1/4$ tspn dried thyme.
1 tablespoon (15 ml) tomato puree.
4 tablespoons (60 ml) red wine or beef stock.
12 oz (350 g) rainbow pasta
(spirals, bows or shells etc).
salt.
pepper.
1 finely chopped spring onion for garnish.

Fry the bacon in a heavy based pan in its own fat until lightly coloured.
Add the oil if necessary, the onion, garlic and green or red pepper and cook until soft. Increase the heat and add the mince. Cook, stirring until it has lost all its pinkness, then add the carrot, thyme, tomato puree, wine or beef stock. Stir then cook over a low heat for 25 minutes until thick.

Meanwhile cook the pasta spials in a large pan of boiling salted water until tender. Drain well. Season the sauce and serve over the spirals.

FILLETS OF SOLE WITH GREEN NOODLES

(Filets de Sole Pochés
aux Nouilles Vertes)

——————— Serves 4 ———————

INGREDIENTS

2 Dover sole, each weighing about
1 lb 2 oz (500 g), skinned and carefully
filleted.
1 small shallot finely chopped.
1 tomato blanched, skinned, deseeded
and diced.
8 fl oz (250 ml) fish stock.
8 fl oz (250 ml) dry white wine.
4 fl oz (100 ml) double cream.
7 oz (200 g) homemade green noodles.
1 oz (30 g) butter.
salt, freshly ground pepper.

Preheat the oven to 190°C/375°F (Gas Mark 5).

Flatten the fillets slightly with a knife blade and fold each one in half, skin side inside. Place them in a well buttered dish and season lightly. Sprinkle the shallot and tomato on top and add the stock and white wine.

Bring to the boil, cover with foil or buttered paper and poach in the oven for 5-10 minutes. Remove the fish and keep warm.

To make the sauce: transfer the fish cooking liquid to a pan and reduce by half. Add the cream and reduce until the sauce is the right consistency. Strain the sauce and liquidise or work with a hand blender until light and creamy. Season with salt and freshly ground pepper.

Meanwhile, cook the fresh noodles in plenty of boiling salted water for 2-3 minutes until 'al dente.' Rinse quickly in very hot water, drain well, toss in the butter and season with salt and pepper.

Arrange the noodles on four warmed plates and place the fish on top. Spoon the sauce around.

Anton Mosimanns

FISH STOCK
(Fond de Poisson)

Makes 1 litre (1³/₄ pints).
2¹/₄ lb (1 kg) broken-up while fish bones
and trimmings.
2 oz (50 g) white mirepoix (onions, white
of leek, celeriac, fennel leaves, dill).
1 oz (30 g) mushroom trimmings.
³/₄ oz (20 g) butter.
4 fl oz (100 ml) dry white wine.
2 pints (1.2 litres) water.
salt, freshly ground pepper.

Thoroughly wash the fish bones and trimmings. In a large saucepan, sweat the mirepoix and the mushroom trimmings in the butter. Add the fish bones and trimmings, white wine and water and simmer for 20 minutes, occasionally skimming and removing the fat. Strain through a muslin or a fine sieve and season with salt and pepper.

HOMEMADE GREEN NOODLES
(Nouilles Vertes)

7 oz (200 g) strong plain white flour,
sieved.
1 oz (25g) fine semolina.
¹/₂ tablespoon olive oil.
1 egg.
a pinch of salt.
2 oz (50 g) spinach purée squeezed dry.
a little warm water.
flour for dusting.

Add the spinach purée, with a little warm water if necessary, to the flour mixture instead of the hot water in the recipe for homemade egg noodles.

Salads

'SALAD DRESSING' ROOM

SALAD DRESSING

INGREDIENTS

2 tablespoons sesame tahine.
2 tablespoons mayonnaise.
2 tablespoons sour cream.
$1/2$ cup (or more) yoghurt.
3 or 4 shallots, diced and fried in butter.
soya sauce to taste.
pepper to taste.
paprika to taste.
cayenne pepper to taste.
1 tablespoon sherry (optional).

David Morse

SUSAN'S SALAD

Serves 2

INGREDIENTS

on a bed of lettuce or chicory.
1 banana chopped.
2 carrots grated.
2 tomatoes sliced.
handful of raisins.
cottage cheese or mild goats cheese.
pineapple or strawberries.
6 almonds.
grated ginger root (optional).
Dressing:
chopped chives and parsley.
walnut oil.
lemon juice or cider vinegar (1 teaspoon).
onion salt to taste.
ground pepper.

Arrange all the ingredients on the bed of lettuce or chicory. Grate the ginger root (if used) onto the cheese. Pour the dressing over.

Susan Hampshire

ARTICHOKE VINAIGRETTE

Anne Diamond

Some vegetables are frankly a luxury and deserve special treatment. The globe artichoke is one such vegetable.

TO PREPARE ARTICHOKES

Wash in cold, salted water. Cut away any stalk and pull off any tough outer leaves.

TO COOK ARTICHOKES

Cook the whole artichoke in boiling, salted water until tender. The time varies from 25 minutes for small, young artichokes, to 40 minutes for very large ones. Test to see if you can pull away a leaf. Drain, remove the 'choke' with the centre leaves.

TO EAT

Allow the artichokes to cool and spoon vinaigrette dressing into the centre. Pull away each leaf. Dip it into the dressing and eat the tender tip.

Pudding

ANNEKA'S RICE PUDDING

Anneka Rice

— Serves 4 —

INGREDIENTS

1½ oz rice.
½-1 oz sugar.
a little nutmeg.
butter as required.
1 pint milk (or mixture of cream and milk
if you're feeling thin!).

Grease a 1½ oz pie dish. Put the rice and sugar in the dish and pour on milk. (I use long rice because I prefer a really milk rice pudding).

Sprinkle with nutmeg and dot with butter.

Place on the second or third runner from the bottom of the oven.

Leave for 2 hours at 170°C (Gas Mark 3).

Serve piping hot with a spoonful of golden syrup!

AMERETTO ORANGES

Kate Mathieson

INGREDIENTS

6 oranges.
ameretto biscuits (macaroons).
ameretto liqueur.
ice cream.
3 egg whites.
6 oz castor sugar.

Cut ⅓ off the top of each orange and retain for decoration. Scoop out inside of orange and discard (we always have chicken and orange salad for lunch on the day after a dinner party, if this is to be the pudding). Freeze the empty orange shells. About 2 hours before serving dinner take oranges from the freezer, roughly crumble an ameretto biscuit into each and then fill to the top with ice cream return to the freezer. Just before serving skewer holes in ice cream and pour in liqueur. Whip egg whites until stiff. add 3 oz sugar. Whip again and fold in remaining sugar. Cover the top of the oranges making sure all the top surface is completely covered with meringue and put in the oven for 2-3 minutes at the highest temperature. Serve on plates decorated with the orange tops and mint or bay leaves (fresh).

BANANA AND TOFFEE PIE

The Rt Hon Margaret Thatcher PM

INGREDIENTS

8 oz short crust pastry.
1 large tin condensed milk.
3-4 large bananas.
½ pint double cream.
2 level teaspoons instant coffee.

Roll out pastry and cook blind in flan dish for approximately 20 minutes on regulo 5. Allow to cool.

Place unopened tin of condensed milk in large saucepan of cold water and cover. Bring water to the boil slowly and then simmer for 2 hours, keeping the tin well submerged in water the whole time. Allow tin to cool.

When cool, open can of condensed milk, which should have turned to a pale brown toffee consistency. Spread toffee mixture on to pastry and slice bananas on to toffee.

Whip cream until thick and add coffee to it until well mixed in.

Spread cream over toffee mixture and serve.

BANANA RAISIN RING

This is a favourite cake of mine, the recipe for which actually came from an elderly Australian friend of the family.

INGREDIENTS

4 oz (125 g) butter or margarine.
6 oz (185 g) castor sugar.
2 eggs.
3 ripe bananas.
$^1/_2$ cup chopped raisins.
$^1/_2$ level teaspoon bicarbonate of soda.
1 tablespoon milk.
1 teaspoon vanilla essence.
6 oz (185 g) self-raising flour.

Cream the butter and sugar. Add eggs one at a time, beating well after each addition. Stir in mashed bananas and chopped raisins.

Dissolve bicarbonate of soda in milk and vanilla essence. Add alternatively with sifted flour to egg mixture. Stir mixture well. Place in a well greased and floured 8" ring tin. Bake in the centre of a moderate gas oven at 350°F/180°C for 30- 40 minutes. When cold, ice with a lemon water icing. Let icing run down the sides.

Nick Faldo

"One of my most memorable meals was one lovely warm summer's eve last year when I barbecued two fresh trout for a family gathering. I just wrapped them in silver foil, having sprinkled them with lemon juice, and coked them to perfection! With just a tossed green salad (must include avocado for me!) and boiled new potatoes with butter and parsley, this made a lovely, simple, summer's supper. Followed by fresh strawberries and cream – what could be better!

The fact that this meal was so special was because it was I who had caught the trout the day before on my first trout-fishing expedition, and I was able to show off my fishing expertise!!"

BARBADOS CREAM

Here is a recipe which I have often made for my family, who all seem to like it, including our three cats!"

——————— Serves 4 ———————

INGREDIENTS

2 small cartons plain yoghurt.
1 small carton double cream.

Whip the cream and mix together with the yoghurt until smooth.

Divide into small bowls or ramekins and top with a thick layer of soft brown sugar.

Refrigerate for at least 2 hours before serving.

BLACKCURRANT MERINGUE

INGREDIENTS

3 oz breadcrumbs.
2 oz soft brown sugar.
½ pint milk.
2 eggs.
8 oz black or redcurrants.
1 oz castor sugar.

Heat the milk and pour it onto the breadcrumbs. Cream the egg yolks and brown sugar, stir into the bread and milk mix and fold in the currants. Pour into a 1 pint ovenproof dish, stand in a dish of water and bake for 40 minutes at Gas Mark 4.

Make meringue in the usual way and pile on top of pudding. Return to oven until brown.

Judi Dench

Ernie Wise

BOB HOPE'S FAVOURITE LEMON PIE

Bob Hope

INGREDIENTS

1 cup sugar plus 2 tablespoons.
3 tablespoons corn starch.
1 cup boiling water.
4 tablespoons lemon juice.
2 tablespoons butter.
4 egg yolks.
pinch salt.
grated rind of 1 lemon.

Combine corn starch and sugar, add water slowly, stirring constantly, until thick and smooth.

Add slightly beaten egg yolks, butter, lemon rind, juice and salt. Cook for 2-3 minutes. Pour into baked shell.

Cover with meringue made from 3 egg whites, beaten stiff, and 2 tablespoons sugar. Bake in slow oven for 15 minutes or until light brown.

THE LEMON PIE SLICE

BREAD AND BUTTER PUDDING

One of my favourite puddings is Bread and Butter Pudding and my wife tells me that she usually makes it as follows:

———— Serves 4 ————

INGREDIENTS

³/₄ pint creamy milk.
2 oz castor sugar.
3 eggs.
4 slices of well-buttered bread, crusts on.
2 oz currants.
a little candied peel (or a little grated fresh lemon rind).
lots of grated nutmeg.

Butter a 2 pint pudding dish, arrange slices of bread, cut in half, over bottom of dish, sprinkle with dried fruit, repeat the layer. Whisk eggs, creamy milk and sugar together, pour over the bread, sprinkle the nutmeg over the top, bake in oven, 350°F/180°C (Gas Mark 4), for about 35 minutes, until top is dark and crispy.

BROWN BREAD ICE-CREAM

INGREDIENTS

4 oz brown bread crumbs.
³/₄ pt double cream.
4 oz icing sugar.
¹/₂ teaspoon vanilla essence.
2 oz granulated sugar.
2 fl oz water.

Crisp bread in oven. Whisk cream to soft peaks, stir in icing sugar and vanilla essence. Freeze for one hour. Dissolve granulated sugar in water and boil for two minutes. Remove and stir in bread crumbs. Remove ice-cream and beat, adding crumbs. Refreeze.

Jim Bowen

The Countess of Dalkeith

CARAMEL PEARS

Diana Rigg

It is delicious and cooked pears are usually so dreary.

INGREDIENTS

2 oz (50 g) butter.
6 tablespoons sugar.
4 ripe pears, peeled, halved and cored.
4 fl oz (120 ml) double cream.
1/2 teaspoon vanilla essence.
2 tablespoons kirsch.

Melt half the butter in a shallow oven-proof serving dish, large enough to take halved pears in 1 layer. Sprinkle dish with half the sugar. Place pears cut side down in dish. Sprinkle with remaining sugar and top each pear with a piece of butter. Bake uncovered in pre-heated hot oven 425°F/220°C (Gas Mark 7) for 20 minutes, basting pears several times with the pan juice.

Mix together cream, vanilla essence and kirsch. Pour over pears and bake 20 minutes longer or until cream mixture is thickened. Serve warm with whipped cream.

KARATE CARMEL PEAR

CHOCOLATE AND CHESTNUT DESSERT

The Rt Hon
Malcom Rifkind QC, MP

This is a very rich dessert, so serve small portions with a biscuit.

———— Serves 12 ————

INGREDIENTS

4 oz butter.
4 oz castor sugar.
8 oz plain chocolate.
few drops vanilla essence.
3 tablespoons liquid – equal parts rum and water or rum and strong coffee.
1 tin chestnut puree.

Cream softened butter, then add castor sugar and beat well together. Put chopped or grated chocolate into a bowl with the liquid and place over steam from pan of water, until liquid. Stir in the vanilla flavouring. Meanwhile, turn the chestnut puree out of the tin and beat with a fork until smooth. Stir the chestnut puree into the butter and sugar until quite smooth, then add the melted chocolate, $\frac{1}{3}$ at a time, until all ingredients are evenly blended. Pour into a prepared tin (as below) and smooth level.

Have ready an oblong loaf tin which has been oiled and place a double band of greaseproof paper at the bottom with the ends coming above the edges of the tin, for easy lifting. Leave the tin in refrigerator until contents have set firmly. When required, turn on to a serving dish and coat with whipped cream (or about 2 oz extra melted chocolate) and sprinkle with shredded and roasted almonds. If liked, the whipped cream can be served separately.

RICH CHOCOLATE MOUSSE

INGREDIENTS

8 oz plain chocolate broken into pieces.
4 eggs separated.
1 tablespoon rum.
$\frac{1}{2}$ oz butter.

Melt the chocolate in a basin over hot water. When melted, stir in the egg yolks, one at a time, the rum and the butter. Whisk the egg whites in a clean, dry bowl until stiff and fold them into the chocolate mixture until thoroughly mixed.

Serve chilled, decorated with whipped cream.

Frankie Howerd

RICH CHOCOLATE 'MOOSE'

CILLA BLACK FOREST TRIFLE

Cilla Black

INGREDIENTS

sponge cake (or any stale cake)
Rowntree's black cherry jelly.
tin pitted cherries.
glace cherries for decoration.
custard powder.
Cadbury's flake.
double cream.
Jordan's apple crunch (alternative).
cherry brandy.

Line the base of the trifle bowl with sponge cake (or stale cake), soaked in the juice from the tin of cherries together with a good dash of cherry brandy (or sherry).

Make the black cherry jelly, pour on top of sponge cake, mix in the pitted cherries. Allow to set.

Make thick custard with custard powder, or for real luxury make an egg custard, pour on top of jelly.

When custard has cooled, whisk up the double cream and pipe on top, sprinkle with Cadbury's flake and decorate with glace cherries.

Jordan's apple crunch is also tasty sprinkled on the cream instead of the chocolate flake.

Serve when completely set.

CRANACHAN

INGREDIENTS

½ pint of double cream.
2 oz oatmeal.
2 oz caster sugar.
1 measure whisky.
4 sponge finger biscuits.

Whip the double cream and the whisky until firm. Fold the caster sugar and the oatmeal. Fill evenly in paris goblets and decorate with sponge fingers. Put in fridge to cool and serve immediately.

CREME BRULEE

Serves 8

INGREDIENTS

1 litre of heavy cream.
1 vanilla bean, split.
9 egg yolks.
90 g granulated sugar.
1 teaspoon vanilla extract.
sugar for caramelising.

Boil the cream with the vanilla bean. Whisk together the yolks and the 90 g of sugar. Pour the boiled cream over the yolks and whisk thoroughly. Remove the bean, scrape out the seeds and add them back into the cream. add the vanilla extract. Pour this cream into 8 individual souffle dishes. Place them in a baking pan and pour cold water into the pan to a depth of half the height of the souffle dishes. Bake for 30 minutes in a pre-heated 175°C oven.

Remove from water bath and refrigerate for at least 6 hours, or up to 3 days. Cream will still jiggle upon removal from oven.

Before serving, cover each creme brulee with a thin layer of sugar, then caramel-ising under a pre-heated salamander.

Capital Hotel, Edinburgh

Head Chef – DOUGLAS MACDONALD
Senior Sous Chef – BREMNER MACDONALD

Dudley Moore

EXTREMELY FATTENING PUDDING

INGREDIENTS

¹/₂ pint double cream.
¹/₂ pint goat's or sheep's yoghurt.
3 dessert spoons dark brown sugar.

Mix cream and yoghurt together very gently with a wooden spoon. Splodge it into a shallow dish, sprinkle it liberally with dark brown sugar (you may need more than 3 spoonfuls).

Put it into the refrigerator for 24 hours. The brown sugar will melt through the creamy mixture marbling it to a browny colour.

Serve with crunchy biscuits – shortcake would be perfect.

Be prepared to make twice as much as people always ask for more.

FRENCH BAKED CUSTARD PUDDING

Serves 4

INGREDIENTS

1 pint milk.
¹/₄ pint single cream.
3 egg yolks.
3 whole eggs.
2 oz castor sugar.
2 tablespoons brandy.

Butter a china ovenproof dish with unsalted butter. Cream whole eggs, yolks and sugar, add brandy, bring milk and cream to the boil and pour over beaten eggs, whisking all the time. Strain into china dish.

Stand the dish in a second container of hot water. Bake at 350°F/180°C (Gas Mark 4) for 35-40 minutes or until set. Cool, chill and serve.

Joanna Lumley

Paul Coia

"I made this once for, a very special lady, who arrived at my house soaked to the skin. I'd been so wrapped up in making it, I hadn't heard her at the door. She'd tramped the district in pouring rain looking for a telephone box to ring me to let me know. I was not popular."

GOLDEN SYRUP SPONGE

— Serve hot —

INGREDIENTS

3 oz sugar.
2 eggs.
4 oz flour.
2 oz butter.
1 teaspoon of baking powder.

Cream butter and sugar, add eggs and flour and baking powder, add a very small quantity of hot water if the mixture is too stiff. Pour into well greased and floured individual moulds or a basin and cover with greaseproof paper and foil and steam or boil for 1½ hours at least.

Serve with warmed golden syrup and custard or cream.

PAVLOVA

— Serve cold —

INGREDIENTS

3 egg whites.
6 oz castor sugar.
1 teaspoon vanilla essence.
1 teaspoon cornflour.
1 teaspoon vinegar.
½ pint double cream.
fruit:
raspberries.
strawberries.
pineapple.
apricots.

Beat egg whites till very stiff – add sugar gradually, continuing to beat until it has dissolved. Add in vanilla, vinegar and cornflour. Spread mixture in an 8" round on greaseproof paper, placed on a baking tray, making sides higher than the centre to form a shell. Bake for 1 hour in a slow oven (Mark 1). Cool, remove carefully and place on a flat tray or board. Fill with the cream (beaten) and arrange drained fruit on top.

Bernard Cribbins

Bonnie Langford

SUMMER PUDDING

Keith Chegwin

Cover pudding basin with slices of stale bread. Gently heat strawberries, redcurrants, blackberries or any other soft fruits in a saucepan with a little sugar.

Strain off the juices and set aside, pour the fruit into the bread-lined basin, cover with more bread.

Place a saucer on the top and a heavy object on top of the saucer. Leave in the fridge overnight.

To serve: invert the basin on a plate and pour the reserved juices over the top.

TURKISH YOGHURT DESSERT

INGREDIENTS

8 oz Greek-style yoghurt.
$1/2$ pint double cream.
8 oz Turkish Delight chopped.
chopped almonds.

Whisk yoghurt gently and fold into cream. Fold in the Turkish Delight. Sprinkle top with chopped almonds.

Can be served in individual dishes or in one large glass dish.

Celtic FC

TULIPE DE SORBET AUX FRUITS D'ETE

(Tulip Basket filled with Summer Fruits and Sorbet)

———————— Serves 4 ————————

INGREDIENTS

3 oz (75 g) tuile mixture.
1 oz (25 g) flaked almonds.
8 oz (225 g) summer berries to include raspberries, loganberries, wild strawberries, blackberries and blueberries.
7 fl oz (200 ml) raspberry sauce.
2 fl oz (50 ml) vanilla sauce.
1 fl oz (25 ml) mango sauce.
6 sprigs of redcurrant.
6 springs of blackcurrant.
icing sugar.
8 fl oz (250 ml) strawberry sorbet.
4 sprigs of mint.

Place an eight-pointed 5 inch (12.5 cm) diameter star-shaped plastic stencil on a buttered and floured baking tray. Spread a little tuile mixture in the centre and draw a palette knife evenly over the surface. Remove the stencil and make three more stars in the same way.

Sprinkle a few flaked almonds in the centre of each star. Bake at 190°C/375°F/gas mark 5 for 4 – 5 minutes until light brown.

Whilst still hot, place each tuile in a small glass bowl to form a tulip basket. Leave in the bowls until cold and crisp.

Divide the raspberry sauce between four plates. Pipe three large spots of vanilla sauce around the edge of each plate. Top each vanilla sauce spot with a small spot of mango sauce. With a cocktail stick, draw through the spots of sauce to give a leaf-shaped effect. Place a sprig of redcurrant or blackcurrant dusted with icing sugar between each.

Place a tulip basket in the centre of each plate and fill with the prepared fruit. Pipe some sorbet into the centre of each tulip basket and decorate with a sprig of mint.

TUILE MIXTURE
4 oz (100 g) plain flour.
4 oz (100 g) icing sugar.
4 oz (100 g) unsalted butter, melted.
2 egg whites.

Sift the flour and icing sugar into a mixing bowl. Quickly stir in the melted butter and egg whites to make a smooth paste. Refrigerate for 30 minutes. Spread the mixture into a stencil to form the desired shape, such as a tulip.

VANILLA SAUCE
18 fl oz (500 ml) milk.
1 vanilla pod.
6 egg yolks.
3 oz (75 g) caster sugar.

Heat the milk and infuse the vanilla pod in it for about 10 minutes. Whisk the egg yolks and sugar together. Bring the milk to the boil, pour on to the egg yolk mixture and mix thoroughly. Place the mixture in a clean pan and stir gently with a wooden spoon over a low heat until the sauce thickens and coats the back of the spoon. Leave to cool, then pass through a fine sieve.

MANGO SAUCE
(Serves 4)

1/2 ripe mango, peeled and seeded.
3 tablespoons peanut oil.
4 tablespoons cider vinegar.
2 teaspoons honey.
1 teaspoon black mustard seeds.
freshly ground black pepper to taste.

Puree mango in a food processor or blender. Add remaining ingredients and process until well combined.

The Savoy Hotel

RASPBERRY SAUCE
10 oz (300 g) raspberries.
2 teaspoons (10 ml) lemon juice.
1½ oz (40 g) icing sugar.
Purée the raspberries in a liquidiser, then add the lemon juice and icing sugar. Pass through a fine sieve or muslin.

STRAWBERRY SORBET
9 oz (250 g) strawberries.
¼ pint (150 ml) water.
4 oz (100 g) caster sugar.
2 teaspoons (10 ml) lemon juice.
Purée all the ingredients in a liquidiser. Pass through a fine sieve or muslin. Freeze in a sorbetière. Alternatively, freeze in a rigid container, then work in a food processor.

Maitre Chef des Cuisines –
ANTON EDELMANN

WEINACHTS CREME

Jayne Torvill

——— Serve cold ———

INGREDIENTS

4 oz granulated sugar.
3 oz walnuts.
4 oz prunes (without pips).
rum.
1/2 pint milk.
2 eggs.
2 yolks.
5 oz castor sugar.
2 drops vanilla essence.
1/2 pint whipping/double cream.

Chop prunes finely, and soak in rum – preferably overnight. Drain excess rum away. Chop walnuts coarsely. Place in pan with granulated sugar over a moderate heat. Stir a few times. When sugar has caramelised and coated the walnuts, pour onto a greased/oiled baking sheet. Leave aside to set before crushing.

Place milk, eggs, yolks, castor sugar and vanilla essence in a bowl. Whisk with an electric beater over a pan of 'just steaming' water. Whisk until thick, and when dripped the drop remains on the surface for 2 seconds. Remove from the heat and continue whisking until cold.

Half whip the cream, and with the prunes, fold into the whisked mixture.

Serve walnut praline separately or sprinkle over at the last minute.

ZABAGLIONE

Francis Wilson

—— Serves 4 ——

INGREDIENTS

4 egg yolks.
75 g castor sugar.
4 tablespoons marsala.

Place the egg yolks in a bowl with the sugar and marsala and whisk them together over a pan of simmering water until thick and mousse like.

Serve immediately.

NOTE: I've found the best way to serve it is in glasses with sponge fingers.

Cakes & Jam

BANANA CAKE

INGREDIENTS

4 oz butter.
$^3/_4$ medium cup sugar.
$1^1/_2$ cups self-raising flour.
$^1/_2$ teaspoon bicarbonate of soda.
$^1/_4$ cup milk.
1 large egg.
3 small or 2 medium sized bananas.

Cream butter and sugar together with a wooden spoon. Mash the bananas with a fork, beat up the egg. Mix all these together.

Sift the flour and bicarbonate of soda and beat into the mixture, adding the milk so that the consistency does not become too dry.

Place in a greased circular ring mould and bake at 325°F for about 1 hour.

When cold the cake can be iced with glacé icing – delicious!

Sir Brian Rix

PEEL A BANANA CAKE
WHAT A FARCE!

CHOCOLATE NUT CAKE

Patricia Hodge

I am passionate about chocolate, but strictly limit myself. However, the power of a really good chocolate cake is hard to resist and this is one of the best recipes I have ever come across.

INGREDIENTS

8 oz margarine.
8 oz icing sugar.
4 eggs.
$1/2$ teaspoon cinnamon.
3 oz grated chocolate.
8 oz ground almonds.
icing:
3 oz plain chocolate.
4 oz icing sugar.
$1^1/_2$ teaspoons nut oil.

Cream the margarine and sugar. Beat in the eggs alternately with the chocolate and almonds. Bake in a 9" farm tin for 45 minutes (about) at 325°F (Gas Mark 4). Leave to cool in tin.

Icing:
Melt the chocolate in a saucepan and stir in the sugar, oil and enough water to obtain the correct consistency. Spread over the cake.

Leave for 48 hours before cutting.

GRANNY MICHELMORE'S RHUBARB CHUTNEY

INGREDIENTS

2 lb rhubarb.
1 lb sultanas.
2 lb demerara sugar.
2 lemons.
1 pint vinegar.
$1/2$ teaspoon cayenne pepper.
1 clove garlic.
1 oz salt.
1 oz ginger root.

Cut rhubarb into shreds, add lemon juice. Bruise the ginger and place in a muslin bag. Cut garlic into small pieces. Put all ingredients into a pan and boil until it is tender and has thickened.

Take out ginger.

Place chutney in jars and keep it corked for a month before using.

SCOTTISH SHORTBREAD

INGREDIENTS

1 lb plain flour.
8 oz castor sugar.
8 oz semolina.
1 lb butter.

Mix all dry ingredients together. Rub in butter. Press into a shallow 10 x 14" tin. Prick all over and bake at 300°F/150°C (Gas Mark 2) for about 1 hour.

Cliff Michelmore

Selina Scott

141

SELKIRK BANNOCKS

The Rt Hon David Steel MP

Makes 2 large bannocks.

———————— Serves 8 ————————

INGREDIENTS

2 oz polyunsaturated margarine.
¼ pint skimmed milk.
2 teaspoons dried yeast.
2 oz soft brown sugar.
8 oz plain flour.
4 oz sultanas.

Warm the margarine and milk to body heat in a small pan, and pour on to yeast in a small bowl. Stir in 1 teaspoon of the sugar, and leave in a warm place until frothy, about 10 minutes.

Sieve the flour into a warmed bowl and stir in the remaining sugar and sultanas. Add the liquid and knead the dough for 5 minutes. Leave to rise, covered, with a damp cloth or polythene, in a warm place until doubled in size, about 1 hour.

Knead the dough again and divide it into two. Shape each piece into a circle and put on an oiled baking tray. Leave them to rise again in a warm place for about 20 minutes.

Preheat the oven to 425°F (Gas Mark 7) and bake for 15 minutes, then reduce the heat to 375°F (Gas Mark 5) for a further 15-20 minutes. Test by tapping the base, which should sound hollow. Cool the bannocks on a wire tray.

WELSH CAKES

Rt Hon Neil Kinnock MP

INGREDIENTS

8 oz/225 g self-raising flour.
4 oz/110 g butter or margarine.
3 oz/75 g currants.
3 oz/75 g castor sugar.
1 large egg.

Rub the butter into the flour. When the mixture resembles breadcrumbs add the currants and sugar. Beat the egg and add to the mixture. Use your hands to make a dough and add a little milk if it is a little too dry.

Now roll the dough out on a floured working surface. Roll it out to about 1¹/₄" (5 mm) thick and cut it into rounds with a 2¹/₂" (6.5 cm) cutter.

Traditionally a heavy griddle is used to cook Welsh cakes but a good solid frying pan will do.

Heat the griddle over a medium heat and cook the cakes for about 2/3 minutes on each side. Make sure they are cooked through and a good golden brown colour.

Serve them as they are or buttered with good Welsh honey.

SORRY, NEIL—THIS ONE LEANS TO THE RIGHT!

BITE INTO A WELSH CAKE!

Snacks

BACHELOR SCRAMBLED EGGS AND TOMATOES

Rolf Harris

– Serves as many as you've eggs for –

INGREDIENTS

2 eggs and 1 tomato per person.
spring onion if liked.
bits of milk.
butter.
salt and pepper.

First melt small splodge of butter (or marg) in frying pan and drop in finely cut up spring onion.

Cook over slow heat for short while, then add a slosh of milk – too much and eggs are watery later. Take pan off heat while you break eggs into pan. Add a dusting of salt to each egg and as much pepper as you enjoy. Then back on to low heat while you graunch up the eggs with a wooden spoon and generally scramble them around.

Must be low heat – nothing is worse than little black horribly tasting burnt bits in scrambled eggs.

Meanwhile your tomato should be cut in half and placed under overhead grill, put flat side down first and grill until skin shrivels up and starts to go black, then turn over, add dusting of salt and grill the flat side.

Your scrambled egg should be just starting to solidify, so take it off the heat for a tick while you pop in your two beautifully grilled tomatoes. The skin on the smooth side just comes away but you will need to cut out the core on the other half of the tomato.

Back on the heat while you squelch up the tomato with the wooden spoon, don't dry it up too much – delicious!

Mix egg and tomato thoroughly.

BEST SANDWICH

2 slices lightly toasted wholemeal bread.
mayonnaise.
lettuce.
slices of cucumber, tomato, avocado.
alfalfa sprouts.
salt and pepper.

Assemble.

CHIP BUTTIE

Take 2 thick slices of crusty white bread. Spread both slices liberally with plenty of butter. Fill with sizzling hot, freshly fried chips.

Season to taste.

Eat immediately!

CORN FLAKES

Buy a packet of cornflakes. Open the cardboard box. Open the sort of plastic packet inside the box. Pour the contents (sort of yellowy brownish bits of things) on to a plate.

Buy a bottle of milk. Take the top off the thin end of the bottle. Invert the bottle gently over the cornflakes, making sure that the milk does not go over the edge of the plate.

It's very simple to make and absolutely delicious. An alternative is to use coca-cola instead of milk. Add basil as required.

Victoria Wood

"My worst meal was when my husband and I ordered 'meringues glacées.' We were presented with 'marrons glacées' which neither of us can stand – loads of them! I had to smuggle them out under my coat!"

Terry Wogan

John Cleese

GOLDEN CRUMPETS

A simple snack and one I use at least twice a week! Two crumpets toasted to golden hue – well buttered (or margarined!) – slice of cheese on each – pop under grill until cheese bubbles – smear or marmite on each and topped with a poached egg a-piece. SMASHING.

PUFFED CHEESE OMELETTE

I'm no expert in the kitchen, but even I can manage to make these delicious omelettes.

INGREDIENTS:

2 eggs.
2 tablespoons grated cheese.
pepper and salt.
1 tablespoon of milk (or water).
$\frac{1}{2}$ oz butter.

Beat the yolks, pepper and salt with the cheese and milk (or water) together. Whisk whites of eggs very stiffly and fold into yolk mixture. Pour into the hot butter in the omelette pan. Stir 2 or 3 times. When set round the edges. Place under a hot grill or in a moderate oven until well risen (7-8 minutes).

Fold omelette over and serve very hot.

Pat Coombs

"Studying at 'LAMDA' (along with Diana Dors, Anton Rodgers and others), we used to frequent a local CAFF(!) in Earls Court, London, after school called 'Jox Box' . . . . None of us could afford more than a cup of tea, but got the sheer joy of hearing the mid-European owner say it, we would offer our wants . . . . and he would shout to his menions . . . . "Fife cups of tea! Unt vun sardine unt tomato sendvich pliss . . . ."!!! (Reckon this true tale comes under 'Happy Days'?).
P.S. I have not tasted a sardine since!!

Joe Loss

"Being constantly on the road with the band, I have enjoyed many special and unusual meals – ranging from a quick sandwich to a feast. However, one that holds special significance occurred in the city of Birmingham during the blitz of the Second World War. We arrived there to play at a local dance hall, only to find that there was no food available for the band. You have to appreciate that these were difficult times, but my wife Mildred, who was with us, wouldn't be beaten. She collected all the ration books from the boys in the band and went all over the city buying whatever food was available. She came back weighed down with the oddest assortment of tins and various packets of food that I had ever seen, and then she set about making us a meal that was truly one of the best any of us had ever eaten. Whether that was because of the circumstances, or the fact that we were all ravenous, I will never know. But I will never forget it."

MUFFIN PIZZA TOPPERS

Jane Irving

—————— Serves 8 ——————

INGREDIENTS

4 tablespoons tomato puree.
2 tablespoons olive oil.
1 tablespoon chopped fresh basil or
1½ teaspoons dried basil.
freshly ground black pepper.
4 wholemeal muffins, sliced in half.
2 beef tomatoes.
4 oz (125 g) Italian salami cubed.
6 oz (175 g) mozzarella cheese cubed.
2 yellow peppers seeded and diced.
salad to serve.

Mix together the tomato puree, 1 tablespoon of the oil and half the fresh or dried basil. Season with pepper. Spread a little of the mixture evenly over each muffin half.

Slice the tomatoes and place one slice on top of each muffin half. Top with cubes of salami and cheese, together with the diced yellow peppers.

Sprinkle each muffin with the remaining basil then drizzle a little of the remaining olive oil over each one.

Place under a hot grill and cook for 3-4 minutes or until the cheese has melted and browned. Arrange muffin pizzas on a platter and serve with salad.

Tips:- Instead of muffins use thick slices of wholemeal bread or crumpets.

For extra Italian flavour, top with anchovy fillets and garnish with black olives.

SELSEY RAREBIT

This is my favourite.

First, take a slice of bread and toast it on one side. Next, spread the untoasted side with butter and then add grated cheese, salt, pepper and anything else you like – I rather favour a bit of chopped onion, or a mushroom or two.

Then toast the 'topped' side until it bubbles. This may sound primitive, but it is excellent.

Clap 2 Selsey Rarebits face to face and you have a MARTIAN PANCAKE!

QUICK SNACK FOR BUSY MOTHERS

I'm no cook but here's a quick snack for busy mothers!

One piping hot toasted crumpet, butter lavishly, then a thin smear of marmite or bovril on top. Top all that with a poached egg. A perfect snack.

Double up for a meal! Children love it – so do I!

Patrick Moore

"This is the 63rd identical request I have had since January. It is getting rather much and I normally send back a 'standard' recipe!! But I am particularly concerned with leukaemia . . ."

Gordon Jackson

"The loveliest meal I ever had was on the landing stage of The Gritti Palace Hotel on the Grand Canal in Venice. I can't remember what I ate – it could have been egg and chips! – but the setting was absoutely memorable!"

Index

COOKING A TO Z

Puddings

Cakes & Jam

Snacks

Buchanan House of Recovery

The Holiday Caring Centre at Buchanan House, for which the book is brought out, is an enormously important creation of the Fund's.

The families of these sick children need to get away together for a holiday much more than most people do; in most circumstances they cannot afford it and so, because of lack of money, they are deprived of these few precious "carefree" days which mean so much to them.

Please buy a lot of the books, give them as presents, get other people interested in them – and interested in all the work the Leukaemia and Cancer Children's Fund has been doing over the years and is continuing to do.

Do think often of these poor little children and help them as much as you can.

Thank you,

Antoinette de Monaco, Mrs John Gilpin.

You'll get it quicker after a pint.

THE CAPITAL HOTEL

Edinburgh
Scotland

A short drive from the historic heart of Edinburgh, the Capital Hotel is set near the slopes of Corstorphine Hill.

It has a restaurant of true distinction. The cuisine has a particular emphasis on Scottish Seasonal Fare, complemented by an attractive selection of Continental and International cuisine.

The Best Things in Life are Coming Back

Clermiston Road, Edinburgh, EH12 6UG.
Tel. 031-334-3391/800 582 8380

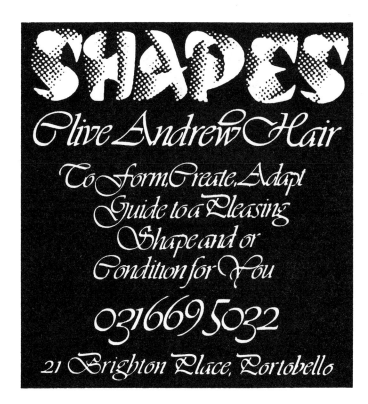

DOLMIO SPAGHETTI BOLOGNESE

1 lb (400 g) minced meat
8 oz (200 g) DOLMIO chilled spaghetti
1 jar (475 g) DOLMIO sauce for Spaghetti Bolognese

Brown mince in a saucepan.

Add jar of DOLMIO sauce to mince and simmer for about 25 minutes. Add water for desired consistency.

Cook DOLMIO spaghetti to packet direction.

Drain spaghetti well, spoon on bolognese sauce and serve.

Serves 4

We all know how deliciously tempting Spaghetti Bolognese is when you use DOLMIO's range of sauces and pasta, but now you can enjoy the delights of their extended selection by trying some of the authentic recipes below!

SOUFFLE FORMAGGIO

2 oz (50 g) soft butter
2 oz (50 g) Parmesan cheese, grated
12 oz (350 g) DOLMIO Formaggio Sauce (frozen)
5 eggs

Grease liberally a 7" (18 cm) souffle dish with soft butter. This is best done by separating soft butter around edge with two fingers to ensure an even coating. Dut with Parmesan cheese and put to one side.

Place Formaggio sauce into a saucepan and bring to a simmer.

Separate eggs, stir yolks into sauce and simmer to thicken. Whisk egg whites until firm and fold into cheese mixture. Turn into prepared souffle dish and bake in a preheated oven at 200°C/400°F (Gas Mark 6), for 20 minutes until well risen and soft in middle.

Serve immediately accompanied by a green salad.

Variations: Spinach Souffle, stir 4 oz (125 g) frozen, chopped spinach into cheese mixture and continue as above.

Carbonara Souffle: Use DOLMIO Carbonara Sauce instead of Formaggio Sauce and proceed as above.

Serves 4 as a starter or 2 as a main course

BOW & PRAWN SALAD

8 oz (225 g) pasta bows or twists/shells
6 oz (170 g) prawns
12 oz (340 g) green beans
4 oz (100 g) sweetcorn
½ (475 g) jar DOLMIO sauce
(original, with mushrooms or with peppers)
1 clove garlic, finely chopped
Pinch of mixed herbs

Cook pasta to pack instructions, drain well and leave to cool.

Cut beans into bite-size lengths and blamch for 2-3 minutes. Mix all ingredients together.

Chill and serve.

Serves 4

Uncle Ben's®

UNCLE BEN's Rice is not only quick and easy to prepare, but it guarantees perfect results every time! Rice contains fibre, minerals, vitamins, protein and is a major source of carbohydrate. Added to this, UNCLE BEN's and healthy eating go hand in hand.

DUCK STIR FRY

8 oz (225 g) UNCLE BEN's Whole Grain Rice
4 Duck breast fillets, skinned and cut into thin strips
4 sticks of celery, cut into 1" (2.5 cm) strips
4 carrots, peeled and cut into 1" (2.5 cm) strips
2 large courgettes, topped and tailed and cut into thin strips
4 oz (100 g) cashew nuts
1 onion peeled and sliced
4 oz (100 g) button mushrooms, wiped and halved
1 tablespoon Suzie Wahn soya sauce (or 1 tablespoon dry sherry)
1 small can of baby sweetcorn, drained
1 clove of garlic, peeled and crushed
Salt and freshly ground black pepper

Fry duck skin in Wok or heavy based frying pan for 4-5 minutes. Discard skin. Stir fry onion and garlic for 2 minutes. Add carrot and celery and cook for further 2 minutes. Add the duck and nuts and stir for a further 4-5 minutes, or until duck is cooked. One minute before end of cooking, add the mushrooms. Add 1 tablespoon soya sauce or dry sherry and season.

Serve on a bed of UNCLE BEN's Rice.

Serves 4

ORANGE RICE RING

4 oz (120 g) UNCLE BEN's Long Grain Rice
1½ pints (900 ml) milk
1 oz (30 g) sugar
3 egg yolks
8 tablespoons orange curd
½ teaspoon mixed spice
15 oz (425 g) can apricot halves in natural juice
4 tablespoons white wine
4 teaspoons Cointreau (optional)

Put rice and milk into a large saucepan and simmer until rice is soft and almost all the liquid is absorbed. Cool slightly and add sugar, egg yolks, 2 tablespoons orange curd and mixed spice. Pour into well buttered 2 pint (1.2 litre) ring mould. Cook in oven 180°C, 350°F (Gas Mark 4), for 20 minutes, or until set.

Drain juice from apricots, turn out rice ring onto a serving plate and fill centre with apricots. In a small pan, blend remaining orange curd with wine and Cointreau, if used.

Serve with rice ring and apricots.

Serves 4

The Complete Quality Package
for all Printing Requirements

Holmes McDougall has a long history in printing and publishing.
Quality, service and expertise are factors which have kept us
to the fore. As label producers we serve many famous names
in the whisky trade as well as industries where the demand is for
high quality labels. We also produce an impressive range
of full colour magazines, calendars, posters, books, newspapers
and commercial print.

24 Clydeholm Road, Glasgow G14 0AU
Tel: 041-954 2121/4 Telex: 777253 Fax: 041-958 0975
137-141 Leith Walk, Edinburgh EH6 8NS
Tel: 031-554 9444 Telex: 727508 Fax: 031-554 4051